Missouri Folklore Society Journal

Special Issue

On Public Folkore in and near Missouri

Volumes 33-34
2011-12

Missouri Folklore Society Journal

(Volumes 33-34, 2011-12)

Special Issue

On Public Folkore in and near Missouri

edited by

Lisa L. Higgins and Jackson Medel

General Editors
Dr. Jim Vandergriff (Ret.)
Dr. Donna Jurich
University of Arizona

Missouri Folklore Society
P. O. Box 1757
Columbia, MO 65205

This issue of the *Missouri Folklore Society Journal* was published by Naciketas Press, 715 E. McPherson, Kirksville, Missouri, 63501

ISSN: 0731-2946; ISBN: 978-1-936135-30-1

Library of Congress Control Number: 2017906197

The *Missouri Folklore Society Journal* is indexed in:
The *Hathi Trust Digital Library*: Vols. 4-24, 26; 1982-2002, 2004. This library essentially acts as an online keyword indexing tool; only allows users to search by keyword and only within one year of the journal at a time. The result is a list of page numbers where the search words appear. No abstracts or full-text incl. (Available free at http://catalog.hathitrust.org/Search/Advanced).

The *MLA International Bibliography*: Vols. 1-26, 1979-2004. Searchable by keyword, author, and journal title. The result is a list of article citations; it does not include abstracts or full-text.

RILM Abstracts of Music Literature: Vols. 13-14, 20; 1991-92, 1998. Searchable by keyword, author, and journal title. Indexes only selected articles about music that appear in these volumes only. Most of the entries have an abstract. There is no full-text.

A list of major articles in every issue of the journal also appears on the Society's web page. Go to *http://missourifolkloresociety.truman.edu/MFS-Jcnts.html.*

Notice to library subscribers and catalogers:
Though the cover date on this volume is 2011-2012, the volume was actually published in 2017.

The Society's board is working to produce enough issues to catch up with the journal's publishing schedule as quickly as possible.

Contents

Introduction (Lisa L. Higgins and Jackson Medel)

The study of folklore in the United States often has led scholars to teaching and research careers in departments of English, Anthropology, and even dedicated departments of Folklore. As students of folklore, we learned that professors like Francis Child, Ruth Benedict, and University of Missouri's H. M. Belden primarily applied their academic training within the classroom to research in the field, and to publication. Then as now, though, many folklorists blurred the lines between the academic and public sector, where folklorists and culture workers also have applied their training. In his career, for instance, Benjamin A. Botkin—professor, editor, field recorder, and head of the Archives of American Folk Song at the Library of Congress—channeled his education and expertise, in what we might now call "folkloristics," toward the public sector. He, and generations since, actively and consciously identified, documented, and then presented "traditional expressive culture" to and for public audiences (Baron and Spitzer, 2007). Professor Belden's contemporary in Missouri, Sarah Gertrude Knott, was trained academically in a different field, in drama, where she acquired vast production skills in community theatre. She then applied those skills and that research to a public sector endeavor, staging the first National Folk Festival in St. Louis in 1934, launching a career that lasted until her 1970 retirement (Williams, 2006). Folklorists now readily claim Ms. Knott as an early leader in our field.

In Missouri, too, we boast a long history of Folklore both in the academy and in the field. Folklorists have over a century of teaching at the University of Missouri's flagship campus, as well as decades at Missouri State University, Truman State University, and Lincoln University. Missouri was also once home to a volunteer-managed, public sector program, Missouri Friends of the Folk Arts. Members of the organization produced festivals under the Gateway Arch in St. Louis; radio programs; and albums like *I'm Old but I'm Awfully Tough*, a collection of old-time music. And the Missouri Folk Arts Program—where the co-editors of this special issue are employed—was founded formally in 1993, after being housed under the auspices of the Missouri Cultural Heritage Center since the early 1980s.

With this rich legacy in mind, we drafted a call for papers, asking for a range of pieces that tell the story of public sector folklore in Missouri. The response was remarkable, and we ultimately worked with authors of the eight articles collected here. From the integration of traditional artists in public school residencies, to collaborations between a folklorist and a social worker who examine foodways, to the personal journeys of a traditional artist and a late-career folklorist, these articles illustrate the partnerships that are created among folklorists, teachers, and professionals throughout the state and region. The works here fall into three broad categories: project overviews and retrospectives; case studies and preliminary fieldwork; and personal narratives.

Amongst the project overviews and retrospectives, we have two articles that directly involve collaborations between folklorists—academic and public—and professionals working in their respective fields. In "Statewide Models for Folk Arts In Education," Susan Eleuterio provides a comprehensive overview of the integration of folk arts into K-12 education, as well as the creation of a set of best practices for the use of folklore, in all its variety, in primary education. In her article, Eleuterio compares the approach that the Missouri Folk Arts Program took in developing curriculum and guidelines to integrate folk arts into the classroom with that taken by North Dakota's Council on the Arts. In these models, Eleuterio emphasizes the collaboration among the professional folklorist, the professional educator, and the traditional artist. Lisa Overholser's article, "The Evolution of Tradition: Preserving Storytelling Traditions with the St. Louis Storytelling Festival," presents the history of the oldest, free storytelling festival in the U.S. Overholser also examines questions of traditionality in the practice of storytelling at the festival and beyond. Not only is the history and formation of the St. Louis Storytelling Festival a valuable addition to the timeline of the traditional arts in Missouri and the country, but this article engages with the ever-present question of what "traditional" means in the world of public performance and print and digital culture. These two articles show the collaborative efforts so central to folklore, the folk arts, and the work that folklorists and artists do.

The second set of articles in this volume focuses on particular case studies and fieldwork projects. Once again, collaborations among folklorists and community members, artists, and experts can also be seen in Rachel Gholson's article "Seeing Traditions & Learning Traditions: Public Sector Work in an Academic Environment." Gholson provides an analytical overview of Jewish traditions in the Ozarks as well as efforts undertaken to educate the community about traditions that exist amongst them but may be overlooked or stigmatized. This multi-phase fieldwork project resulted in a large collection of materials, multiple scholarly papers, and the creation of numerous public events. Where Gholson walks the line between case study and project overview, the following two articles tend more towards the case study model. Mariah Marsden's "Ozark River Storytelling: Social Networks, Narrative, and Courtship in a Modern Rural Festival" presents a picture of traditional narrative storytelling within a small group. Marsden describes her experience participating in a spontaneous storytelling event among her own family group, an autoethnographic overview of a quasi-public "festival." Marsden ultimately focuses on a particular tale that demonstrates some of the key themes and functions of the narratives themselves within the small community. Claire Schmidt, folklorist, and Laurel Schmidt, social worker, co-author a similar type of preliminary case study in "Foodways and Resistance in a Missouri Residential Mental Health Facility." Dr. Schmidt and Ms. Schmidt present various ongoing efforts amongst the staff to improve both eating habits and staff-client relations. This joint effort between a folklorist and a mental health professional interrogates the patterns of consumption and social hierarchy amongst the staff and clients. A regional educational effort; a locality-based spontaneous narrative event; and a collaborative ethnographic study: each of these projects brings folklore into the public sphere at different levels, demonstrating the valuable observations that team efforts and investigations can yield for groups, organizations, and institutions.

The final section in this issue is more narrative in its focus. Willi Goehring provides an example of the blending of narrative and ethnographic study with "The Politics of Transference in Traditional Fiddling: A Narrative Case Study." The author narrates his own process of engagement —as outsider, folklorist, and participant—with a traditional Ozarks fiddler and craftsman in Arkansas. Goehring develops a clear view of the process of his apprenticeship to and appreciation of regional master artists. Gladys Caines Coggswell illustrates both sides of apprenticeship, from her experience as an apprentice and as a master artist. In "Reflections on Public Folklore from a Traditional Artist," Coggswell represents the traditional artist's viewpoint, not only as she participated in Missouri's Traditional

Arts Apprenticeship Program, but also as that participation led to a variety of opportunities to perform, learn, and teach. Finally, an interview with Howard W. Marshall nicely rounds out this special issue. Tracy Anne Travis, a Masters student in Folklore at the University of Missouri, spoke with Dr. Marshall about his personal and professional history in folklore and folk arts, including the work he has done in "retirement" and his long view of the field. These narrative projects provide useful and compelling examples of the ways that representation is useful, even central to folklore practices, works, and history.

We co-editors sent out our call, asking for a diverse range of papers, and we received a remarkable sampling of essays representing historical and contemporary public folklore efforts in Missouri. Herein, we see a broad scope of what folklore is and what it does in the collaborations between members of many sectors within, and beyond, the field. Our understanding of the public sector, here, is not limited to conventional definitions of festivals or events. Our understanding of the public sector is intentionally broad and inclusive. Additionally, scholarly and creative efforts bring the folklorists and their stories into the conversations among teachers and learners, workers and community members. As folklorists working in the public sphere, we see these kinds of interactions on a regular basis and these articles clearly demonstrate the strength of public folklore in Missouri. Similarly, there are a number of ongoing projects across the state that demonstrate the same ideas, and due to a number of conflicts, including space and time, those projects and their leaders are not represented in this special issue. Dr. Norma Cantu and her students have been pursuing fieldwork in Kansas City with Latino populations and their traditions, as well as presenting some for the public, and we look forward to the forthcoming special issue of this journal on Latinx and Chicanx traditional culture in the Midwest. Professional folklorists, like Rachel Reynolds Luster and Matt Meacham, and local culture workers, like Kathleen Morrissey, Marideth Sisco, Jim McFarland, and Paula Speraneo, have produced a wide array of folklife projects and fieldwork in West Plains, Mo. The staff, instructors, and volunteers of the Folk School of St. Louis have grown a fairly-new program into a vibrant one. Folk Alliance International has moved to Kansas City and expanded its programming beyond the celebrated annual conference to include public projects like the KC Folk Fest. Grassroots and local projects have been conducted by community scholars and local culture experts in communities like Bethel and Sugar Creek for decades. Indeed, the power of folklore to reach out to communities, and the ability it has to empower local community members and professionals, is fodder for at least one more special issue of the *Missouri Folklore Society*

Journal. We hope that someone takes up the mantle and edits a second, or third, edition for our edification, and for posterity.

Finally, we would like to thank our colleagues at the Missouri Folk Arts Program, Dorothy Atuhura and Tracy Anne Travis, graduate assistant and graduate intern, respectively, both of whom took the time to review and proofread the articles collected here. Thanks also to the leadership of the Missouri Folklore Society for inviting us to co-edit this collection.

Works Cited

Baron, Robert and Nick Spitzer. *Public Folklore.* Oxford, MS: University Press of Mississippi, 2007. Print.

Williams, Michael Ann. *Staging Tradition: John Lair and Sarah Gertrude Knott.* Champaign, IL: University of Illinois Press, 2006. Print.

Statewide Models for Folk Arts In Education (Susan Eleuterio)

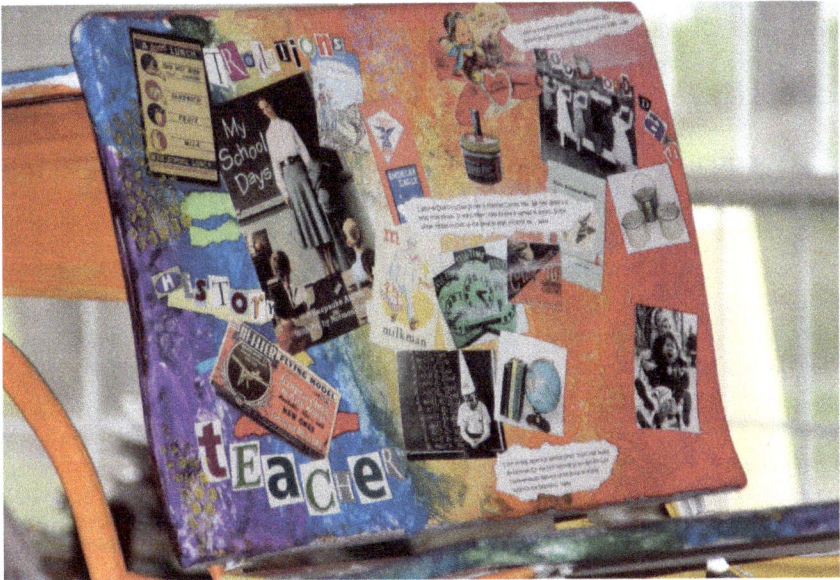

Desk Collage North Dakota Art for Life (photo courtesy Jennifer Parker, Executive Director, Nelson County Arts Council)

Public folklorists have been interested in collaborations with K-12 educators and folk and traditional artists ever since Benjamin Botkin described the work of Rachel Davis DuBois using the model of an applied "parranda,"

1

or house party, to promote intercultural learning and understanding.[1] In *Through the Schoolhouse Door*, Lynne Hamer and Paddy Bowman provide an important overview of the work of DuBois and other folklorists and educators such as Dorothy Howard during the 1930s and 40s, along with a thoughtful analysis of the history of folk arts in education programs (FAIE) in the United States up to the present.[2] While FAIE programs have been initiated in nearly every state of the US, many of them remain short lived due to a variety of issues including lack of funding, the transient nature of employed folklorists who must often go where the jobs are, and the pressures of state and national mandates focused on test scores rather than hands-on classroom experiences with tradition bearers.[3]

One model which has been developed to address some of these issues is designed to provide curriculum and lesson plans focused on the specific cultural practices of artists living in a state or region, in order to provide educators with easy-to-use materials aligned with state standards and curricular goals. The Missouri Folk Arts Program developed a statewide curriculum targeted to elementary school teachers, which also provided background material on collaborating artists who were available for school residencies.[4] This essay compares this model with that of North Dakota's Council on the Arts program which developed documentaries on folk and traditional artists in collaboration with Prairie Public Broadcasting. The documentories have accompanying lesson plans as well as enhanced CDs produced by NDCA. In both cases, the author, a professional folklorist and educator, worked in collaboration with folk and traditional artists, a professional public folklorist based at a state arts council, and additional personnel (including staff from community organizations, professional ed-

---

[1] Eleuterio, unpublished MA Thesis, "Folk Arts In The Schools: A Closer Look," 1983, quoting Benjamin Botkin in "Applied Folklore: Creating Understanding Through Folklore." *Southern Folklore Quarterly*. 3. (September 1953). p. 204.

[2] *Through the Schoolhouse Door*, Introduction, pp. 1-18.

[3] Bowman and a number of other folklorists and educators, including the author, were brought together at a roundtable on Folk Arts in Education in 1993 by the National Endowment for the Arts and City Lore to examine the role of Folk Arts and Education. These same issues (funding, state and federal mandates focused on other areas, etc) were noted at the time. While one of the recommendations described in a report issued afterwards (*Folklore in the Classroom, Changing the Relationship between Schools and Communities* by P. Bowman and S. Zeitlin, 1993) has since been established (creating a clearinghouse of information and resources) and is now called "Local Learning: The National Network for Folk Arts In Education" (www. http://locallearningnetwork.org), statewide programs in folk arts in education have either been eliminated or marginalized, as have many arts in education programs with the recent rise of statewide budget cuts and increased emphasis on STEM.

[4] Missouri's Folk Arts in the Schools program, which preceded the development of the curriculum guide is described in "From 'Show-Me' Traditions to 'The Show-Me Standards:' Teaching Folk Arts in Missouri Classrooms." See Higgins and Eleuterio, pp. 120-138, in *Through The Schoolhouse Door, Folklore Community, Curriculum*.

ucators and others) to design classroom-ready lessons.

This review of the models begins with an overall description of each program, followed by notes about lessons learned based on oral conversations with Troyd Geist, the state folklorist with the North Dakota Council on the Arts, and with Carmen Dence, a Colombian dancer, choreographer and the founder of Grupo Altantico of St. Louis, Missouri. The conclusion examines some lessons learned and possible strategies for future statewide models of curriculum and program development.

Lisa Higgins, folklorist and Director of the Missouri Folk Arts Program (MFAP), in our co-written history of the Missouri Folk Arts Residency Program, underscores the need for creating FAIE projects which are "organic, individually crafted for each occasion, relevant to the 'climate' and culture of the locale, and never rushed." She likens this to the "slow food movement,"[5] which is a concept contradictory to the rush and pressure of most public educational environments, where, as Troyd Geist notes, "the educational system seems to go through cyclical changes that require readjustment. I think this constant readjustment is detrimental to gaining a foothold and long-term impact. It constantly puts us back at square one."[6]

The first phase of Missouri's FAIE project (which began in 2005) followed over 15 years of educational programming by MFAP with elementary students and was designed to co-create long-term school residencies by three master traditional artists: African American educator and storyteller, Gladys Coggswell; folklorist and fourth generation fiddler, Howard (Rusty) Marshall; and Colombian dancer, choreographer and costume maker, Carmen Dence. My role during this phase was to provide professional development workshops and feedback for the artists on working with school culture, developing long term residencies in schools, and creating lesson plans with outcomes geared to the Missouri Department of Elementary and Secondary Education's standards in six content areas, and state performance goals.

As we noted in our published Case Study of the project, after the first phase of our FAIE residency program in response to evaluation and assessment, participating teachers "indicated that they felt inadequately prepared to host the residencies in regard to content, they wanted to be able to prepare themselves and their students before the artists arrived at the school to plan and execute residencies."[7] The second phase of the program therefore focused on the creation of a statewide curriculum with lesson

---

[5]Higgins, "From 'Show-Me' Traditions to 'The Show-Me Standards:' Teaching Folk Arts in Missouri Classrooms," p. 128.

[6]Geist Interview. May, 2016.

[7]Higgins and Eleuterio, p. 128.

plans, titled *Show-Me Traditions; An Educator's Guide to Teaching Folk Arts and Folklife in Missouri Schools.*

The guide, which is available on line at *http://mofolkarts.missouri.edu/-publications.shtml* was developed during 2007 and 2008, including being pilot tested during a residency by folk artist Carmen Dence at two rural elementary schools.[8] In addition to the pilot residency, a number of additional folk and traditional artists participated in another series of professional development workshops on developing school residencies and in co-creating lesson plans for the guide. These artists, many of whom had also participated in Missouri's Traditional Arts Apprenticeship program, included bluegrass musician and instrument maker Bernard Allen; Ozark riverways specialist and jonboat builder Don Foerster; Irish harpist Eileen Gannon; cowboy poet Dan Hess; German bobbin lace maker Linda Hickman; square and jig dancer/caller Cathy Davis Marriott; spoken word poet Maria Guadalupe Massey, African-American percussionist Wayne Robinson; and African American storyteller Angela Williams. In developing statewide models, one goal has been to include the range of cultures represented across the state; from rural to urban, from locally based place traditions and practices such as Ozark riverways boatbuilding to folkways imported and maintained (or in some cases, revived) by immigrants—such as German lace making, Colombian dancing, and Irish music—to uniquely American mixtures of culture such as African American storytelling and drumming. By presenting these artists, art forms, and the cultural context they represent, the guide offers teachers and school communities an opportunity to learn more about the local and to explore the rich variety which exists within state borders.

A team of educators, folklorists, and folklore graduate students including Julie Hale, the Arts Education Program Specialist for the Missouri Arts Council, Deborah Fisher, the Executive Director of the Missouri Alliance for Arts Education, and Deborah Bailey, a folklorist with the Missouri Folk Arts Program, participated in the workshops on developing residencies and materials for schools. They were instrumental in making sure that the guide included curriculum connections to grade level expectations (or targets for instruction) as well as to Missouri's Show-Me-Standards, the name for the state standards which are still referenced today under the Missouri Learning Standards (*http://www.missourilearningstandards.com/about/*) as "the knowledge and skills students need in each grade level and course for success in college, post-secondary training and careers."

As a number of folklorists who work in and with schools have noted, partnerships with arts educators provide a number of benefits. First, they

---

[8] A detailed description of this residency is given in *Show Me Traditions* on pages 128-137.

provide access to the knowledge base of working with schools and teachers through AIE programs, which, unlike FAIE programs, have tended to be more consistently funded and staffed at state arts councils.[9] Secondly, they help to address what Lynn Hamer and Paddy Bowman call "the invisibility of the field of folklore in this country."[10] Finally, they are important because the folklorist who is working at the state level in creating FAIE programs is frequently not a K-12 educator and almost always has many other job responsibilities in addition to developing school programs. As Troyd Geist noted in our interview, "Even when you are wearing the FAIE hat, you may or may not have direct control over funds."[11] Along these lines, we emphasized in our description of the MFAP that: "Arts administration professionals at state and local agencies are a key link between teachers and the resources needed to enrich classroom learning.[12] In particular for this project, Director Higgins employed connections between MFAP and the Missouri Association of Community Arts Agencies (MACAA) a statewide network of community arts agencies, in connecting the guide, artists, and resources with local schools interested in adding folk arts to their curriculum and programs.

In addition to field tests of the lessons at Clarence and Shelbina Elementary schools, a committee of folklorists and elementary school based educators reviewed the entire guide and provided feedback. A key aspect of developing the guide which I believe to be a best practice for creating any curriculum materials (including lesson plans) is this collaboration not only with artists and folklorists, but most significantly, with classroom teachers. As a former classroom teacher, folklorist in the schools, folk arts coordinator and current educational consultant, I can attest to the perpetual churn of expectations, jargon, approved methodologies, and staffing at public schools. For folklorists who are trained to first study the organizational culture of environments and the people who work in them, trying to pin down school culture is difficult. Every time a principal changes, a state adopts new standards, or as is often the case lately, pressure increases for teachers to teach to the test, the standards—which as Bowman and Hamer

---

[9]Bowman notes in her essay, "I Didn't Know What I Didn't Know," that the Arts Education Partnership (AEP) developed at the same time as specific standards for arts education were being established (45-46). In the same volume, Bowman and Hamer underscore the connections which can be made as well with music educators, the National Council for the Social Studies, the National Art Education Association, and the National Council of Teachers of English. "Conclusion: Learned Lessons, Foreseeable Futures." In *Through The Schoolhouse Door* (217-225).

[10]Bowman and Hamer, p. 223.

[11]Troyd Geist, Interview, May 2016.

[12]Higgins and Eleuterio, p. 138.

point out[13] have become the hook for folklorists to make a connection to curriculum expectations—become less relevant unless a case can be made for direct impact on teaching and learning.

The guide was designed to address specific questions raised by the project classroom teachers. It begins with *Defining Folk Arts and Folklife,* which includes sections on reasons for teaching folk arts and folklife; defining folk culture; introducing students to folklife; and using family stories and folk songs to teach research, language, speaking skills and to foster awareness of cultural traditions and folk culture. Next comes *Discovering Folk Arts In Everyday Life* which includes lessons on family folklore, material culture, traditional dance and festivals, oral traditions and foodways. And finally the guide includes a section with profiles of the folk artists who participated in the project along with learning outcomes and resources for preparing ahead of time for bringing the artist into the classroom. The guide was published in print in 2009.

Once the guide was completed, we conducted outreach to local teachers at two regional events in 2010: the Festival of Nations hosted by the International Institute of St. Louis, and the Ozark Studies Symposium hosted by Missouri State University. These events showcased the artists who are featured in the guide. Arts council administrators who were part of MACAA assisted by contacting local teachers and encouraging them to participate. Thirty-five educators participated at the St. Louis event and twelve educators attended the Ozark Studies Symposium.

An electronic edition of the guide with revisions was published on the MFAP website in 2011. Later that year, the Folklore and Education Section of the American Folklore Society awarded the guide the Dorothy Howard Folklore and Education Prize, which "recognizes projects that encourage K-12 educators or students to use or study folklore and folkloristic approaches in all educational environments."

Meanwhile, I returned to the Chicago area. While I have stayed in contact with the MFAP staff and several of the artists who participated in the program (social media platforms such as Facebook have drastically improved the ability of all of us to stay in communication on a regular basis), as our funding ended, both I and the MFAP staff turned to other areas of focus.

While we did not conduct any official evaluation (time and money once again being the issue), I would argue that the project goals—

- Provide professional development and support for folk and traditional artists to design and present long term residencies in schools,

---

[13]Hamer and Bowman, p. 218.

- Address needs of K-12 classroom teachers (particularly those who teach local history at the elementary school level) through a teacher's guide designed to address subjects in folk culture tied to statewide folk and traditional arts and culture, and

- Conduct outreach through community arts organizations to develop partnerships with schools, artists and the Missouri Folk Arts Program,

were clearly achieved. Of the twelve artists who participated in the program and were listed in the guide, five (or nearly 50%) are currently listed under Arts Education on the Missouri Arts Council's roster of Missouri Touring Performers for 2016. This listing includes the opportunity to present their art form as part of the Missouri Arts Council's monthly programs throughout the state and/or to participate in programs designed by communities and schools with funding under the Missouri Strategic Performing Grants category. As we noted in our write up in *Through The Schoolhouse Door*, a number of issues impact the ability of traditional folk artists to participate in touring rosters, especially for school based programs. These include the fact that they are often not full-time artists, with "day" jobs which preclude school programs. Moreover, Missouri (and many other states) requires teaching artists to spend a minimum amount of time in school, and in terms of touring, scheduling demands make it difficult to travel outside their home area.[14] Given these limitations, a 50% retention rate of artists in the program over a six year period is encouraging.

The guide is now listed on the Local Learning website *http://locallearningnetwork.org/regional-resources/* under "Regional Resources for Mid-America," which means hopefully teachers not only in Missouri, but across the region may access it to learn more about using folk arts and folk culture in the classroom and specifically those based in Missouri traditions and culture. It would be interesting and helpful to know how many times it has been downloaded from either the MFAP or the Local Learning site as a quantitative source of evaluation.

---

[14]Higgins, Eleuterio p. 122.

With Sue Eleuterio's able instruction, public and private funding, and dedicated Missouri Folk Arts Program (MFAP) staff time, several traditional artists trained to present in-school residencies and to design curricular materials grounded in their traditions and informed by MAC's Art Education guidelines. MFAP then parlayed strong relationships with local arts councils around Missouri into a few curated residencies. Eleuterio and I worked hand-in-hand with the artists and local arts council directors, who provided direct links to the best, and most receptive, classroom teachers. The combination of all these partners led to successes.

Eleuterio and I witnessed or overheard stories about isolated students who found community, if only for the week of the residency, as well as students who engaged with class content more enthusiastically. I recall a story about a new immigrant student in rural south central Missouri whose attendance was typically sporadic but attended every day when Colombian dancer Carmen Sofia Dence was on campus. We also heard from parents in northeast Missouri whose children not only had answers to the nightly "how was school?" question, but readily demonstrated what they learned from Dence or old-time fiddler Howard Marshall. Middle school students in central Missouri were so engaged with traditional storyteller Gladys Caines Coggswell during her residency that they pooled their meager allowances to send flowers and get well cards to Coggswell when she suffered a stroke shortly after the residency.

With the cadre of artists and feedback from teachers, we also designed a teachers' guide that we hoped would help teachers welcome traditional artists into the classroom. We provided vocabulary, lesson plans, and worksheets. We connected each lesson to Missouri's Grade Level Expectations, as well as the state's published objectives and outcomes. I was determined, when proposing the project, to bring traditional artists into Missouri schools in substantive ways, beyond the occasional Friday concert in the gymnasium. Ultimately, MFAP abandoned the formal Folk Arts in Education project due to obstacles, especially with regard to time and access. The residencies are exceptionally labor-intensive for staff, artists, and teachers, and standardized testing obligations reduced the amount of time available for residency planning and implementation. With evolving educational standards, our teachers' guide rather quickly became dated. And, as will happen, artists and MFAP staff were diverted by new opportunities. Still, working with Sue Eleuterio, the traditional artists-in-residence, and the teachers at select Missouri public schools created some of the most rewarding, and exhausting, experiences of my career. Happily, a few of those artists still apply their folk Arts in Education training in classrooms and other educational settings. — Lisa L. Higgins

In order to learn more about the project's impact on the participating artists, I spoke with Carmen Dence, with whom I have stayed in touch since the guide was published. Ms. Dence has recently retired from her day job as an Associate Professor in the Department of Radiology at Washington University Medical School in St. Louis.

Folklorists in state programs frequently provide technical assistance to artists, and the relationship is mutual. This can take the form of advice from the folklorist on grants available to individuals and communities, mentoring in accessing non-specifically-folk-arts aspects of promoting their work, and vice versa for folklorists in the specifics of cultural practices. In 2014, Carmen and I co-wrote an essay on Colombian food in America for *American Ethnic Food Today: A Cultural Encyclopedia*.[15] We have also maintained the relationship which was created through our participation in the MFAP program, becoming "friends" on Facebook, connecting through LinkedIn and more recently thinking out loud together as Carmen pondered where to take her passion and advocacy for Colombian dance and culture.

As evidenced by this one example, in creating and sustaining statewide FAIE programs, one theme which repeatedly comes up is collaboration. Writer and activist in nonprofit cultural and community development work, Tom Borrup, quotes Arthur Hillelman: "collaborating is a relationship in which each organization wants to help its partners become the best that they can be at what they do."[16] I would argue that collaboration is also a relationship in which each individual in an FAIE program, whether folklorist, K-12 teacher, artist, student, parent, principal, arts administrator, community member, etc., wants to help each become the best they can be at what they do, and at the same time, *to expand their concept of "what they do."*

As we noted in the *Show Me Traditions* guide, "Family and local culture are often the first things we learn. ... all children in America learn about local and state history as part of their educational curriculum, but history is often taught in isolation from what children learn at home. By tying folk arts and folklife into the regular curriculum, you can show students and their parents that there are connections between their own cultures and those of people around the state. These lessons are designed to help your students meet state educational standards and expectations. These lessons are also designed to help your students use their homes, neighborhoods, and even schools as living laboratories. Arts and culture programs in the

---

[15]Dence, Carmen with Eleuterio, Susan. "Colombian American Food," in *Ethnic American Food Today: A Cultural Encyclopedia.* 2015.

[16]Borrup, Tom. *The Creative Community Builder's Handbook*, p. 155.

classroom have been proven to bolster student self esteem, to introduce teachers to methods that reach their students' multiple intelligences, and to engage parents and family members in their children's learning."[17]

Carmen describes some of the ways MFAP's program achieved this for her as an artist, teacher, and community member:

> The (MFAP) program got me focused in a more structured way when I'm creating something now. It helped me focus on how to look for information, and it helped me learn what is important when you are working with non-Hispanic groups. I've always said it's great to go to an all Mexican, or all Central American community (to teach). They are going to learn something new, but the MFAP programs and residencies brought forth what is more important and critical when I am addressing non-Hispanics. I want to bridge that gap of knowledge that we have from and of each other. Doing a folk arts residency dance program at Edison Theater in St. Louis a few years later, I realized if I was going to make a dent in race relations, I have to go out of my Hispanic comfort heritage. As I am teaching, I am also learning from their backgrounds. I can't tell you the number of times someone from Japan or India will say, "we have a dance with some similarity to this dance story." It's like a big world family.

> As a consequence of doing that work in 2012 in St. Louis, I created what is now the "Dancing Damsels." They are a group of dancers from ages 55-85 years old. They come the first and third Saturday of every month. They have other artistic talents: some of the most accomplished are an African-American dancer-choreographer; another one (from Germany) is the first violinist in the St. Louis Orchestra, and one more (also from Germany) is a singer in the St. Louis Chamber Chorus.

> The other thing that impacted me was how the kids when they came to the (MFAP) program talked to their parents. Their parents were living in an isolated tiny community, and they got feedback from the kids and showed up. When they saw the kids dance in the program, it was with glowing faces, an expression of "we never imagined this." You knew when you worked with the kids, that you were working with the family, indirectly educating them, you know they are going to talk about what they saw. The lesson was that what happens in

---

[17]Eleuterio and MFAP staff, *Show Me Traditions*, p. 2.

the classroom, any classroom (and my house is a classroom for dancers), has no borders.[18]

Carmen Dence. (Photo by Dana Everts-Boehm)

Today, Carmen finds that most of the requests for her programs come for single day workshops. She notes:

---

[18]Interview with Carmen Dence, May, 2016.

This is not the same as doing a residency, but perhaps it's a bit more comfortable for (teachers) in an urban city school—doesn't disrupt. They don't have to make the emotional adjustment (of a sustained residency program) for two hours, half a day. You have a conversation and then it's "good-bye." However, you don't have the emotional bond with the students that you do in a residency. The pros and cons are obvious and something is better than nothing, but we need more curriculum development, more face-to-face and interactive evaluation, and really bringing the traditional arts to the same level of process (in schools) as with any other fields. It's still a battle. When you have the longer time with one classroom, then you have the satisfaction of almost one-to-one conversation, more time to answer their questions and even question their questions. That's something I love to do, which helps to clear the preconceived ideas the students may have about the presenting artist, including his/her origin, nationality, cultural and educational experience."[19]

Although there is still more to be learned about the impact of the *Show Me* educator's guide on educators in Missouri, one direct impact of the MFAP program was to inspire a similar program in North Dakota through the North Dakota Council on the Arts (NDCA) Folk and Traditional Arts Program.

In 2007, Lisa Higgins and I presented as part of a panel on public folklore about the Missouri model at a folklorist retreat. One of the participants, Troyd Geist, the Director of the North Dakota Folk and Traditional Arts Program, was interested in our model of co-developing curriculum with folk and traditional artists and wrote a grant in 2008 to bring me to North Dakota. As in the Missouri model, we began with three traditional artists who were master artists in their respective traditions: Dakota/Hidatsa storyteller, community scholar and educator (and National Heritage Fellow) Mary Louise Defender Wilson; Southeast Asian Indian artist and scientist, Nandini Katti; and Southeast Asian Bharatanatyam dancer Margaret Sam. Each had been identified by the Folk Arts Program as being interested in creating portfolios as residency artists for the NDCA's Artist in Residence Program. Through a series of face-to-face workshops we held in North Dakota along with correspondence via email and phone, each of the artists created a residency program including specific lesson plans, resources, illustrations of art work, ideas for culminating activities, and connections to ND State Standards.

---

[19]Ibid.

All three of the artists successfully applied to the NDCA Artist in Residence Roster, which was one of the goals of our program. An additional goal was to increase the participation of traditional artists in this program by being listed on the roster. In North Dakota, an independent panel of education specialists reviews all proposed new artist applicants. That panel praised the materials and plans of the three new folk artists with whom we worked. In addition, Nandini Katti was hired in the fall of 2009 as a science teacher using Asian Indian folk arts to teach science as her curriculum. Nandini credited this to the training she received from our program. At that time the NDCA's two most prominent Arts in Education Programs were Artist in Residence and Teacher Incentive. For Artist in Residence, the percentage of program funding that went to support folk artists ranged anywhere from 24%-33%. The percentage of program funding in Teacher Incentive that supported folk arts was as much as 50% in some years. Then changes in education and arts education occurred and a steady decline began. Troyd noted, "These education changes happened some years after the training."

As in Missouri, the second phase of this project (which took place from 2009-2011) became a collaborative exercise in co-creating lesson plans with artists, namely folklorist Troyd Geist, and Linda Ehreth, the Arts Education Director for NDCA. In this case, rather than a single curriculum guide, a series of on-line guides for teachers were developed to support teaching and documentary material which NDCA Folk and Traditional Arts had created with several partners, including Prairie Public Broadcasting, Makoché Recording Company, Spirit Room Gallery and the North Dakota Public School Libraries. (Copies of all of the documentary CDs were donated to every North Dakota Public School Library.)

Beginning with Mary Louise Defender Wilson, we produced a series of lessons to provide support material for an enhanced CD based on the traditional story *The Woman Who Turned Herself to Stone*. The guide is designed to provide teachers with lessons for classroom pre-listening, listening, and post-listening to the CD. As in the case of Missouri, North Dakota folklore and arts education staff wanted to make sure that teachers felt they had contextual material which explained the connections between students' own lives, folk culture, and everyday experiences as well as connecting to the North Dakota Standards and Benchmarks for grades 4-8. *http://www.nd.gov/arts/resources-services/traditional-arts/documentaries*[20]

---

[20]This link is connected to all of the lesson plans, documentaries, and enhanced CD's described in this section. The Prairie Public documentaries for Keith Bear, Mary Louise Defender Wilson, and Norik Astvatsaturov can also be found at North Dakota Studies, a collaborative website of Prairie Public, the North Dakota Humanities Council, and the State Historical Society of North Dakota at *http://www.ndstudies.org/media/prairie_artists_-*

As a team, we developed four additional guides, including a second story told by Mary Louise Defender Wilson, *The Blue Heron Who Stayed for the Winter* (from the enhanced CD *My Relatives Say: Traditional Dakotah Stories*) which again includes pre-listening lessons, lessons for using the CD in class, and post-listening lessons, all tied to ND Standards and Benchmarks.

In 2010, I worked directly with the artist, Mandan and Hidatsa storyteller and flute player Keith Bear, to create lesson plans tied to a traditional story, *Turtle and Pretty Crane*, which he tells on the NDCA produced CD, *Morning Star Whispered,* along with a documentary video produced through Prairie Public Television. NDCA AIE Director Linda Ehreth facilitated professional development for this workshop using a reflective protocol called descriptive review.[21] This process underscores collaboration, listening, and questioning—all qualities of both of the statewide programs described here.

For the other two guides, I worked with Troyd to create lessons based on the documentaries about additional artists. *A Lyrical Life: The Struggle and Hope of South Sudan* introduces students and teachers to the culture, history, music, and dance of the Ma'di people of southern Sudan and northern Uganda. They are represented by four Sudanese musicians: Remis Silvestro, Ijjo John Stephen, Samuel Dau, and Peter Majak, who came to North Dakota to flee the wars in South Sudan. As in the Missouri program, each of these artists also participated in the NDCA Folk and Traditional Arts Apprenticeship Program.

We also produced a teacher's guide to accompany *God Given: Cultural Treasures of Armenia,* which showcases the work of Armenian metal *repoussè* artist, Norik Astvatsaturov. Formerly of Baku, Azerbaijan, he is now an American citizen in Wahpeton, North Dakota. Like the four young Sudanese musicians, Astvatsaturov was forced to flee his homeland as a refugee, but has maintained centuries old traditions in his new home.[22]

As with the Missouri FAIE program, once the project was completed and the funding cycle ended, I returned home and the material began a life of its own. I have continued to collaborate with Troyd from time to time, most recently in creating a lesson plan on nicknames for a program called *Art for Life*[23] which NDCA Folk Arts developed beginning in 2001

---

keith_bear_turtle_and_pretty_crane.

[21]Ehreth along with other arts educators developed a reflective teaching model for teaching artists to develop and examine their work. C alled "Artist to Artist," it can be found here: *http://opd.mpls.k12.mn.us/Artist_to_Artist2.html.*

[22]*www.ndstudies.org/media/prairie_artists_norik_astvatsaturov_god_given_cultural_treasures_of_-armenia*

[23]More about this program can be found here: *http://www.nd.gov/arts/programs/art-for-life.*

to specifically address what have been called the "three plagues of living in elder care facilities:" loneliness, boredom, and helplessness.[24] This program, which is ongoing, first paired local arts agencies with eldercare facilities to bring intensive and extensive arts and artist interaction with the elders to help improve the elders' emotional and physical health by addressing the Three Plagues. As this partnership solidified, a third partner was brought into the fold, that being local elementary schools and schoolchildren. Troyd and I discussed the impact of the original FAIE program and its connection to NCDA's Folk Arts programming.

He noted:

> FAIE seems to be only possible at the behest of structure and focus of educational institutions we work with, and ... those institutions, the stipulations, benchmarks/standards, and approach to their goals seems to change every 5 years. If we want to work within those structures, we constantly have to readjust to those cyclical changes- not only to that but also to funding issues and transitions. Since it takes 2 years to get going, because of grant funding, we end up looking at 18 months of trying to align or realign with school systems, and that puts you 3 ½ years into their cycle and there's another change. Since the focus in arts education changes so often, for us, (as folklorists) we need to help train traditional artists to work with educational institutions, which also takes time. All that leaves a very short window of opportunity where we can be effective. Or we can search for another "outside the box" way of having that impact as we have done with the school component of the Art for Life Program.

At the same time, Geist has seen a positive impact from the state based professional development for artists and curriculum materials we developed:

> These materials and the training helped folk artists to become more comfortable in educational institutions so they are more comfortable taking up the opportunity to participate. In terms of the curriculum materials and the videos- the key is to be flexible with them- just like our fieldwork- good material from fieldwork can apply to so many things. They may not sit perfectly with what we intended but they are a good foundation for being creative. For instance, with what I'm doing as the

---

[24]Geist, letter to author, June 2013.

state folklorist- I can't really count on being able to control as much as I would like to in arts education. So I try to tie it into existing programs such the Arts for Life Program. We match up arts agencies with local elder care faculties and within that funding we have been able to have them partner with schools, so the schools are now part of a tripartite partnership. By focusing on certain grades, (4th /8th- where the curriculum emphasizes local social studies), we have the kids do an art interaction with the elders through the subject matter of North Dakota studies. The benefit to the school is they meet their goals (state standards) and we don't have to deal with other programmatic requirements that the school teacher may find overly rigid. The Art for Life Program is a program that I control in my budget that I can help shape consistently and on an ongoing basis.

In that program, we are currently working in 12 towns, and for each town, we have a school component. For instance, last week- in Aneta (a small town with only 222 people) the 7th grade students got together with elders at the local care facility. The elders and the students exchanged and compared stories about their nicknames, their first day of school, school life (such as saying the Pledge of Allegiance). The teaching artists, David Paukert and Robert Kraft, got an old school desk from the 1930s. The artists along with the elders and schoolchildren took that information, painted the desk, and created a collage turning the desk into a piece of art that spans the decades and reveals how things have changed and how they remain the same. The desk resides at the eldercare facility as a piece of art. (*See illustration at the beginning of this article.*) The greatest thing we can do is to try to get people to see how what they do connects to something. Traditional artists, when referring to their practice, often say that it is just something they do. They may not, initially, have a conscious perception of their practice as an art, so we are getting them to recognize their important role as an artist, and then getting them and others in various institutions to see and understand how their tradition can positively impact what they do—whether it's working with kids, working with elders, or working with teachers. Education programs and their changes come and go, but the folk and the value of what they bring to the table remains constant.[25]

---

[25]Geist Interview. May, 2016.

Lessons Learned and Still to Be Examined

Statewide classroom-ready lesson plans and teaching materials about folk and traditional arts can be created through thoughtfully designed partnerships with folklorist/educators, teachers, state and regional folklorists who are not education specialists, folk and traditional artists, and arts education specialists—things which endure beyond a single funding cycle, and through the power of the Internet, beyond the borders of any one state arts agency. Key to successful materials which will be used in the classroom is the inclusion of classroom teachers in each stage of the process.

Both quantitative and qualitative evaluation needs to be conducted to document if, how, and when these materials are being used by classroom teachers, within the state, and if possible, regionally, since many art forms and cultural groups exist across political borders and boundaries.

In spite of the push for Common Core standards,[26] state educational leaders continue to develop state specific standards and benchmarks which include a focus on local history, culture, and people. Also despite the continued pressures of nationalized testing, which cut into time previously allocated in many of these programs to arts inclusion, teachers still have to cover the material outlined in state standards. While budget cuts, testing schedules, and attrition mean there are fewer windows of opportunity for teachers to engage with folk and traditional artist residencies, these changes may also mean they are looking for classroom-ready lesson plans which provide direct connections to the culture and traditions of their students' families and communities, and to the state as a whole.

Conclusion

As Troyd Geist points out, the first strategy for developing this type of program is to be flexible. In both cases, the state folklorist was willing to use preliminary responses and evaluation by classroom teachers to adapt the types of programming from one which was artist based to one which was classroom based. The second strategy, as both Lisa Higgins and Troyd Geist have noted, is to think of this work as similar to the "slow food movement," where locally sourced and indigenous materials (and in this

---

[26] One year ago, the Missouri legislature voted to ban the statewide tests tied to the Common Core standards. *http://www.stltoday.com/news/local/education/missouri-legislature-throws-common-core-test-out-the-window/article_09441f40-b77a-5f0d-ae9f-7678a30d551a.html* North Dakota's legislature has also considered banning the so called Smarter Balanced test which is tied to the Common Core.

case, artists and traditions) are valued, time is permitted to develop outcomes which are mutually important to all parties involved, and to quote Carmen Dence, "we bridge the knowledge gap we have from and of each other." Finally, to return to the theme of collaboration: those of us who are teachers and ethnographers are more convinced than ever that successful education is a dialogue, not a monologue.

A challenge for folklorists and their allies is to identify funding, time and partners who see the value of folk and traditional arts in K-12 schools and curriculum. One possibility for the future use and development of FAIE curriculum and lesson plans are hybrid programs where state and/or regional folk arts coordinators work in concert with university programs, both in folk culture and in education. Oregon, Ohio, Missouri, Kentucky, Wisconsin, Indiana, and Michigan have all created or are developing collaborations between public folklorists, university-based folklore programs, and in some cases, such as Missouri, state arts councils. In addition to sustainability of funding, undergrad and graduate level students can be engaged in assisting with the field work needed to identify artists, art forms, and cultural practices which can be included in future curriculum models. Creating FAIE programs which are true partnerships can make for sustainable statewide programs which provide an opportunity for everyone to be lifelong learners.

Works Cited

Borrup, Tom. *Creative Community Builder's Handbook: How to Transform Communities Using Local Assets, Arts, and Culture*. 2006. Fieldstone Alliance.

Bowman, Paddy and Lynne Hamer. Editors. *Through the Schoolhouse Door: Folklore, Community, Curriculum*. Logan, UT. Utah State University Press. 2011. Print.

Higgins, Lisa L. and Susan Eleuterio. "From 'Show-Me' Traditions to 'The Show-Me Standards:' Teaching Folk Arts in Missouri Classrooms." In *Through the Schoolhouse Door: Folklore, Community, Curriculum*, 120-138. Logan, UT. Utah State University Press. 2011. Print.

The Evolution of Tradition: Preserving storytelling traditions with the St. Louis Storytelling Festival (Lisa Overholser)

Abstract

In this article, I will present a historical perspective on the traditional storytelling basis of the St. Louis Storytelling Festival. Given that the Festival and its precedents were originally conceived of, planned and produced with some members of Missouri Friends of the Folk Arts, including MFFA founder and Missouri state folklorist Barry Bergey, who went on to become the NEA director of Folk and Traditional Arts, the topic is particularly relevant to the special issue. Additionally, the article provides an opportunity to review the history of SLSF and publish for posterity. The article will open with questions about notions of the "traditionality" of storytelling, the growth of professional storytelling, and the Festival's role in storytelling in Missouri.

Introduction

The St. Louis Storytelling Festival recently celebrated its 37th Festival on May 4-7, 2016. Produced by the University of Missouri Extension Community Arts Program, the event featured storytelling sessions, workshops and public storytelling events across the St. Louis Metropolitan region. In 2016, as in each year prior, the Festival presented a talented roster of storytellers performing at different types of venues and settings, including schools, libraries, parks, historic sites, outreach locations for specific audiences, and performance venues. Since the Festival originated through the University of Missouri-St. Louis Continuing Education Department, and continues today through the University of Missouri Extension Community Arts Program, the Festival is inherently designed for outreach and engagement with the public. From this perspective, the Festival as a tool of public education and service bears similarities to the goals and intentions of public sector folklore, the prime focus of this article.

When I became the new Director of the St. Louis Storytelling Festival in December 2014, the Festival was in the midst of a major upheaval as it was in the process of transitioning organizationally from the University of Missouri-St. Louis Continuing Studies Department to the relatively new Community Arts Program within University of Missouri Extension. Amidst it all, the Festival Advisory Council and I forged ahead with Festival planning, and despite these major organizational changes in the background, the 2015 was still scheduled to occur as planned in early May 2015, a mere five months after I took the helm as Director of the Festival / Urban Region Community Arts Specialist with MU Extension. There was little time to fully absorb or appreciate the historical scope of the Festival, aside from basic initial research into the its origins. For the next several months, I was consumed entirely with the most immediate, critical concerns of Festival production in an administrative framework I was myself new to. When the dust finally settled sometime in the summer of 2015, whatever breathing time I had newly gained was used to become more thoroughly trained in the procedural ins and outs of a major University administrative system as planning for the 2016 Festival soon ramped up once again.

As an Extension Faculty member and as a trained folklorist, I also could not ignore the fact that right around this time, major—indeed historic— events were happening on the University of Missouri-Columbia campus. Protests on the campus in fall 2015 spilled over into a national spotlight, by nature affecting the University's real and perceived relationship with the surrounding communities in a very tangible way, putting those of us who work in community engagement and outreach for the University in a historically unique situation. For me personally, as with all of us in Extension, it caused me to reflect and to wonder what I could do, how I could be of service in my position to communities. My work as Festival Director and Urban Region Community Arts Specialist does not require me to work as a public sector folklorist, yet many of the tools in my professional toolbox utilize the same principles and methodologies I acquired in my academic training as a folklorist/ethnomusicologist and in my job as a public sector folklorist with the New York Folklore Society. These tools suddenly seem more relevant than ever.

These thoughts were on my mind as I produced the 2016 St. Louis Storytelling Festival, and now that it is over, I find myself with a good opportunity to reflect upon these conceptual interconnections and steep myself in understanding the Festival's history. As the Festival nears its 40th anniversary, I realize it does so amidst a backdrop of immense social, cultural, and technological change over the previous four decades that have redefined the nature and role of storytelling in society. This article will provide a basic historical overview of the St. Louis Storytelling Festival, examining the relationship to traditional storytelling and public folklore at the Festival's inception, the Festival's ongoing evolution within and alongside this traditional framework, and new opportunities for meaningful public sector engagement.

The St. Louis Storytelling Festival

The first St. Louis Storytelling Festival occurred in 1980, co-founded by Ron Turner, who was Dean of the University of Missouri-St. Louis College of Arts & Sciences Continuing Education Division, and Lynn Rubright, a professional storyteller and educator who at that time was teaching at Webster University and had developed PROJECT TELL (Teaching English Through Living Language) in the Kirkwood R-7 School District. The Festival was co-produced with the Jefferson National Expansion Memorial National Historic Site (JNEM), and the events were primarily held on the grounds of the Gateway Arch, an iconic symbol of westward expansion and of the historical and cultural heritage of St. Louis. The Festival Planning Committee represented a number of different organizations and institutions, including JNEM, UMSL, the Collaborative for Experiential Learning, Clayton School District, the Kirkwood R-7 School District, the Jewish Federation of St. Louis, and The Seven-Up Company (one of the sponsors of the Festival).

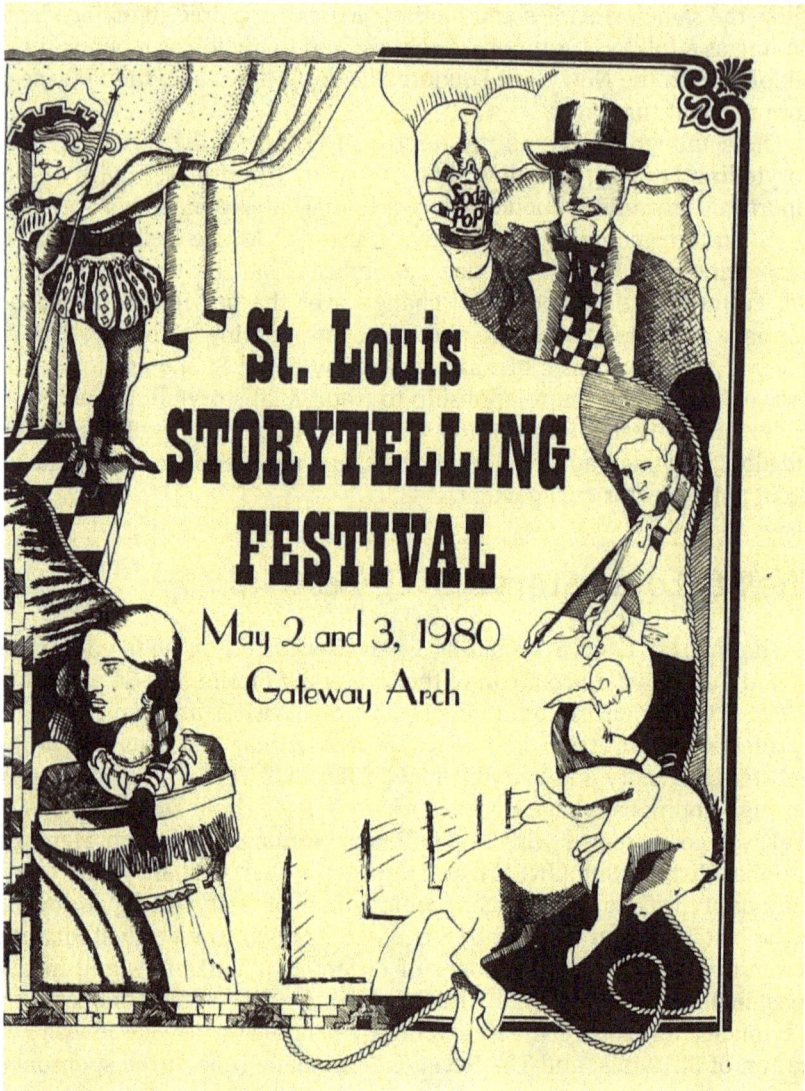

Image 1: The 1980 St. Louis Storytelling Festival Brochure, graphic by Susan Mathews

Planning meeting notes from November of 1979 reveal discussions that centered around the how, what and why of producing a storytelling festival. In reading through these notes, what is most evident to me is the noted desire for the Festival to reach out to communities outside of the Festival institutions, as well as the idea that storytelling could be used as a way to engage with various St. Louis communities, as evident in notes listing potential Festival Program Objectives, a sample of which I list below:

- "To help people gain an appreciation of the rich cultural heritage surrounding St. Louis as the past and future Gateway to the West"
- "A storytelling festival under the Arch makes the statement that humans pass on their personal and cultural heritage orally"
- "To develop multi-ethnic awareness; the Arch symbolizes that reality"
- "To tell each other the real stories of our lives"
- "To give children experience in telling their own stories"
- "To give older people an outlet to tell their story"

Other comments reveal the idea that storytelling (and story listening) is a powerful educational tool, both inside and outside the classroom:

- "To demonstrate the use of story-telling as an analytical method for both social studies and literature classes"
- "To provide a forum for the discussion & interpretation of storytelling styles, origins & techniques"
- "Storytelling is a pleasurable experience that captures the imagination, as well as informs & delights the listener"
- "To participate in an experience in which wisdom sharing (being silly is a form of wisdom) is fun"
- "To arouse the conscience level of individuals and organizations to the varied amount of ethnic heritage that is present"

Ultimately, the informal mission statement that was printed in the Festival brochure included many elements and ideas from the previous planning comments:

> The St. Louis Storytelling Festival seeks to encourage the recounting of life experiences and the preservation of cultural and historical heritages. It attempts to fulfill the human need, particularly strong in a modern urban environment, for reflection on the human experience that comes through in a unique way in storytelling. Through hearing and telling stories, we may develop awareness of basic commonalities, individualistic perceptions and styles. Stories, like museums, are a link with the past; but they are also a vigorous voice of the present. For the Jefferson National Expansion Memorial and the University of Missouri-St. Louis, presenting the storytelling festival is another way to make history a viable and meaningful experience for the visitor and to encourage individual involvement in an ancient tradition. (1980 Festival Brochure, p. 5)

Clearly, the Festival was seen as a tool of community engagement, as a way of educating the public about the rich cultural, ethnic and historical heritage of St. Louis. The idea that Festival planners wanted to encourage others in St. Louis to share their own stories is a nod to the notion that storytelling is a dynamic way to encourage sharing of the lived experiences of their own communities, and to connect institutional artifacts to still-living traditions and experiences. This is not unlike what public folklorists do – and it's not by chance. The St. Louis Storytelling Festival was a specific genre-focused event that was actually a small part of a larger contextual whole. That contextual whole involved a series of forces that came together in the 1960s and 70s to align storytelling and public folklore in some very specific ways.

The traditional roots of the Festival

The first St. Louis Storytelling Festival program included mostly professional storytellers (e.g., Lynn Rubright, Jay O'Callahan, and Emily Thach) alongside a handful of traditional storytellers (Glenn Ohrlin, Tim Tallchief). This distinction was not formalized in the program itself, but must be made because it underscores the inherent duality that has been present with the Festival since its founding. On the one hand, the brochure refers to storytelling as an "… ancient tradition," and notes that "..(s)tories, like museums, are a link with the past, but they are also a vigorous voice of the present"—casting storytelling in a very traditional light. An additional two pages of the brochure relay a brief history of storytelling that begins with the following: "Storytelling is one of the oldest means of human communication," immediately establishing the ancient connection to the past that defines so many other traditional expressions. On the next brochure page, a brief paragraph describes "The Folk Tradition," referring to storytelling as "… a folk art with roots deep in the tradition of myriad religious, ethnic, and regional groups." And even in the brochure's "Suggestions for Further Reading" (yes, this is also included in the brochure!), a folklore reference book is listed, Catherine and John T. Flanagan's *American Folklore: A Bibliography, 1950-1974*.

On the other hand, the brochure verbiage that serves to establish a traditional basis of storytelling is also knowledgeably counterbalanced with other sections which make clear that not all storytelling is necessarily "traditional." The section called "Storytelling Today" clarifies that "Today's storytellers come from all walks of life, culture, and occupational backgrounds. Librarians, actors, housewives, business men and women, grandparents, teachers, senior citizens, children, city dwellers, and country folk all tell tales," and goes on to say that only "(s)ome storytellers are 'traditional tellers.' They tell stories that reflect and come from the culture in which they were raised." Through these statements, Festival planners were clearly aware of the distinction.

Indeed, there is no claim that the Festival itself is exclusively traditional. But the strong and overt effort to highlight the traditional nature of storytelling (which continues in promotional materials for the Festival even to the present day), and the usefulness of storytelling as a traditional form, does have precedence, thanks to the work of public folklorists.

Public sector folklore in St. Louis and the United States as backdrop

The most immediate local precedents for the St. Louis Storytelling Festival were the folklife programs that happened at JNEM in the late 1970s with Jane Grogsby Bergey, Curator of Folk Arts from 1975-1983 under JNEM superintendent Robert Chandler, and the Missouri Friends of the Folk Arts, a non-profit organization founded by Barry Bergey, then Coordinator of Student Activities at Washington University.

Jane Grogsby Bergey had been working and performing at Focal Point, a local coffeehouse that tended to have a lively folk music scene at a time when the folk music revival was still going strong. A new, "visionary" superintendent at JNEM heard Jane perform and offered to hire her to come to JNEM as a Folklife Coordinator in 1975; there she performed and programmed musicians and other traditional artists to help in the work of interpreting themes of JNEM. For example, at the Museum of Westward Expansion exhibits, artists from cultural groups who were represented in the exhibits, such as Native Americans, Mexican Americans, cowboys, fur trappers, and voyageurs were scheduled to perform to demonstrate the living traditions of these groups. At the Old Courthouse, where the Dred Scott decision was rendered, she programmed many traditional African-American artists and musicians, gospel singers, etc.

Simultaneously, Barry Bergey had formed the non-profit Missouri Friends of the Folk Arts (MFFA) in St. Louis, dedicated to researching Missouri's folk arts traditions. MFFA sponsored the first Mississippi Valley Folklife Festival in 1976 at Washington University, with support from the Jefferson National Expansion Historical Association, the National Park Service, and the Missouri Arts Council. One year later, over Labor Day Weekend in 1977, the Festival continued on the grounds of the Arch, and in 1978, it was renamed the Frontier Folklife Festival to tie it more closely to themes of the site. Like the other folklife programming Jane had been conducting at JNEM, the goal was to present the traditional artists in connection with site themes.

For the Festival, the model they followed at JNEM was very much in the same vein as the National Folk Festival, which coincidentally got its start in 1934 as a product of the newly formed National Folk Festival Association (today called the National Council for the Traditional Arts, or NCTA) under the leadership of native St. Louisian Sarah Knott. In terms of public folklore, the National Folk Festival was a milestone. It was the first multicultural traditional arts celebration in the United States, and it shaped the format of staged folklife presentation for years to come. For the first time, scholars were presented on stage with the folklife practitioners as presenters; folklife talks and demonstration workshops became a festival fixture, and craftspeople were invited to do demonstrations as a kind of performance, among other firsts. Additionally, not only did many of the performers on those early stages become the greats of the folk arts performance scene in subsequent years, but the Festival also employed some of the earliest public folklore fieldworkers, including notable figures like William Bascom, Richard Dorson, Ben Botkin, and Zora Neale Hurston. ("A Brief History of the National Folk Festival") The Festival rotated locations every few years, but it once again found a home in St. Louis in 1947, where it remained until 1955 when it found other itinerant Festival homes.

These presentation modes were carried out and utilized at the Frontier Folklife Festival. A range of disciplines and cultural groups were represented - some examples include rancher, singer and cowboy poet Glenn Ohrlin; St. Louis bluesman Henry Townsend; Ozark singer Almeda "Granny" Riddle; French fiddlers Joe Politte and Charlie Pashia from the Old Mines area; and French Canadian Cajun musicians Mark Savoy and Dewey Balfa from further south along the Mississippi in Louisiana. Missouri Friends of the Folk Arts helped by doing some of the fieldwork and documentation necessary for public sector work, while JNEM and the NCTA helped provide administrative and staffing support. Notable is the fact that some of these individuals, such as Glenn Ohrlin, were also skilled storytellers as well, and often told stories as part of their presentations at the Frontier Folklife Festival and other traditional interpretive programs at JNEM. They were not professional storytellers, but Jane Grogsby Bergey soon realized through seeing a performance of Lynn Rubright's one-woman storytelling show "Pioneer Woman" that non-tradition, "interpretive" storytelling was just as useful and appropriate for her interpretive programs.

The Storytelling Revival

All of this happened just as a new storytelling movement, the storytelling revival, was burgeoning. To understand the rise of professional storytelling, one need not travel any further than Jonesborough, Tennessee, home of the National Storytelling Festival, and the International Storytelling Center. For the small town of Jonesboro (*the name was later changed to the present-day Jonesborough), passage of the National Historic Preservation Act was a major impetus for revitalization of the downtown historic area, and a Jonesboro Civic Trust was formed to implement these plans in 1970. According to storyteller and folklorist Joseph Sobol, an enthusiastic member of the Trust by the name of Jimmy Neil Smith was imbued with a historical preservationist ethos. Amidst the civic celebrations that surrounded the revitalization efforts in Jonesboro, the story goes that he had by coincidence heard a story told on the radio one day about coon hunting in Mississippi (as told by Jerry Clower, a Grand Ole Opry performer), and suddenly conceived of the idea of an entire festival centered around storytelling. He brought the idea to the Trust, who acquiesced and gave him a small grant to produce the festival himself, and the first National Storytelling Festival was born in 1973.

This is generally considered to be the main catalyst for the storytelling revival movement, and it spread like wildfire, giving rise to the occupation of the "professional storyteller." Given that the profession had not really existed as such until then, and that storytelling previously had come from a more traditional foundation, it was inevitable that tensions arose between what was considered "traditional" storytelling and "professional" storytelling.

Tensions Arise

Joseph Sobol, in his dissertation on the contemporary storytelling revival movement, characterizes this tension by referencing Anthony F. C. Wallace's classificatory schemes of revitalization movements in general. He first describes in Wallace's own words three of the "subclasses" of revitalization movements—the "nativistic," the "revivalistic," and the "vitalistic:"

> "Nativistic movements" ... are revitalization movements characterized by strong emphasis on the elimination of alien persons, customs, values, and/or material from the mazeway ... "Revivalistic" movements emphasize the institution of customs, values, and even aspects of nature which are thought to have

been in the mazeway of previous generations but are not now present ... "Vitalistic movements" emphasize the importation of alien elements into the mazeway ... (Wallace, p. 267, quoted in Sobol, p. 14)

He then goes on to apply this to the storytelling movement:

According to this classificatory scheme, the revitalization movement gathered under the term "storytelling revival" contains a mixture of revivalistic, vitalistic, and nativistic elements. Though most storytelling enthusiasts' cultural programs emphasize the revival of an artistic mode presumed to have had greater currency and influence in an ideally imagined past, many tellers are also eagerly importing traditions and repertoires that had no part in their own particular backgrounds. Still others are performing nativistic exercises, selectively representing in their storytelling the traditions of their own ethnic ancestors, yet often, quite naturally, wielding those traditions on behalf of explicitly contemporary political and cultural programs. Political friction between the nativists and borrowers has even manifested itself on the storytelling scene, coming to a head at the second National Storytelling Congress in 1988, where meetings on the theme of ethnic traditions erupted in recrimination and defensiveness between the two camps. (Sobol, 14-15)

Loosely, if we equate the "nativistic" camp with traditional storytelling, since it involves tellers drawing upon their own ethnic ancestral traditions, and the "vitalistic" in particular with those who do not, since it involves the "importation of alien elements," or experiences drawn not just from their own, but from another's ethnic ancestral experiences, and then performing that on stage (in a professional capacity, typically for compensation), the questions arise: is that cultural appropriation? And what are the implications for public folklore? Arguments can be made either way, and it is not my goal here to provide an answer one way or the other or to delve into this question here. I only detail the particular frameworks and issues as they relate to storytelling and public folklore.

In my to-date short-lived experiences as Director of the St. Louis Storytelling Festival, I know these conversations have been had amongst the storytellers, organizers and audience members in St. Louis, though I don't know many specifics. And what I have uncovered in research tells me that the traditional backdrop of the St. Louis Festival matters because at one time, care was taken to distinguish the two, and to accurately represent and characterize when traditional storytelling happened at the Festival, and when it did not.

Though obvious, perhaps, it is important to remind ourselves that the St. Louis Storytelling Festival is not a "Folklife" Festival. Although a range of cultures and traditions are typically represented, the Festival is not implemented with the same kind of ethnographic fieldwork one would find at a public folklife program; folklorists are not on stage with presenters, and there is typically not a range of other traditional demonstrations or activities happening (though the Festival does have a history of music and dance performances included in Festival programs). It has traditional roots, and many of the same people who were involved in JNEM's folklife programming in the late 70s and early 80s were also on the St. Louis Storytelling Festival Planning Committee.

The Future of Storytelling Traditions at the St. Louis Festival

In conclusion, as I ponder what this research about the traditional roots of the St. Louis Storytelling has taught me, and the ways in which public folklore and public sector folklorists have crossed paths with the Festival, a few thoughts come to mind:

1. The Festival has maintained the connection with JNEM over the years, and has even widened its scope to presenting storytellers at lots of other institutional venues as well, including the Missouri Botanical Garden, sculpture parks, science centers, and hospitals. Keeping in mind that the storytelling festival was originally envisioned as a way to help in interpretive efforts at JNEM, the same integrity that public folklorists use in this setting can be applied to interpretive efforts elsewhere. There is a lot of room for this to happen, and the same "toolbox" can be used.

2. Just as the Festival at one time allowed institutions like the University of Missouri-St. Louis and the Jefferson National Expansion Memorial to expand their reach into communities with greater opportunities for public engagement, communities continue to transform and change. Demographics not only change, but the issues affecting communities also evolve and change. If storytelling is to help communities tell their own stories as Festival planners had originally

intended, then work needs to be done to uncover what stories communities WANT to tell. In many ways, the Festival's new home with Extension is an ideal place for the Festival to be for this kind of work.

3. Storytelling itself has also evolved, and new forms and settings for storytelling are changing as well. In particular, the open-mic storytelling movement, characterized by its emphasis on personal, true-life stories and authenticity of storytelling, has its own unique history (which is the subject of another article). Digital storytelling is another method that needs to be considered; and there are others. In 2016, the St. Louis Storytelling Festival presented a program in collaboration with Second Tuesdays, a monthly open-mic storytelling gathering, to explore the ways they could work together. Additionally, St. Louis seems to be home to a rich variety of verbal forms, including spoken word, slam poetry, rap, and so on. Public folklore work could be very useful in uncovering these particular histories and traditions that have as yet not been presented at the Festival.

Works Cited

Abrahams, R., Cantwell, R., Davis, G., Green, A., Griffith, J., Hawes, B., Siporin, S. (2007). *Public Folklore* (Robert Baron & Nick Spitzer, Eds.). University Press of Mississippi.

Bergey, Jane Grosby. (1978, Feb.) Mississippi Valley Folk Festival. In *Courier (The National Park Service Newsletter)*.

Hollen, Chris Van. (2014, Nov. 19). Tribute to Barry Bergey. *Capitol Words*. *http://capitolwords.org/date/2014/11/13/E1565-3_tribute-to-barry-bergey/* Accessed May 31, 2016.

Moore, Bob. (1984, June). Chapter nine: Museum services and interpretation. in S. Brown (ed.) *Jefferson National Expansion Archival Documents*. *https://www.nps.gov/parkhistory/online_books/jeff/adhi2-9.-htm* Accessed June 1, 2016.

National Council of the Traditional Art. (2013). A brief history of the National Folk Festival. Retrieved from *ncta-usa.org/a-brief-history-of-the-national-folk-festival*.

National Storytelling Network Website, *http://www.storynet.org/*.

The St. Louis Storytelling Festival Committee. (1980). The St. Louis Storytelling Festival Brochure.

Sobol, Joseph Daniel. (1994). *Jonesborough days: The National Storytelling Festival and the contemporary storytelling revival movement in America* (Vols. 1-2). Evanston, IL: Northwestern University. Dissertation.

Wallace, Anthony F. C. (1956). "Revitalization movements." *American Anthropologist*, 58: 264-81.

Seeing Traditions & Learning Traditions: Public Sector Work in an Academic Environment (Rachel Gholson)

Telling Traditions/Seeing Traditions existed as a ten-year (2003-2013), dual phase project designed to document the Jewish communities of the Ozarks region and to create multiple educational products in the course of the research process. The project entailed a collaboration of researchers— Mara Cohen Ioannides, a community scholar, and Dr. M. Rachel Gholson, Folklorist and Associate Professor of English at Missouri State University (MSU). The project melded both academic and public sector folklore approaches, resulting in the following outcomes:

- Compilation of over 1,400 still images

- 60 hours of video footage, documenting temple and family life over a full year

- Creation of a web site focusing on Jewish traditions and life in the Ozarks housed by the Ozarks Studies Institute (*http://ozarksstudies.-missouristate.edu/tellingtraditions/*)

- The creation of a documentary focusing on the roles of women in the community, entitled *Home, Community and Tradition: the Women of Temple Israel*

- Acceptance of this documentary for showing at the "New York International Independent Film and Video Festival," at the "Warsaw Jewish Film Festival," at the International Oral History Association meeting in 2004 and at the American Folklore Society meeting in 2005

- The creation of the Ozarks Jewish Archive at Missouri State University, Springfield, Missouri

- Receipt of funding from the Community Foundation of the Ozarks for a photographic display

- The *Seeing Traditions* photographic display and display booklet

- The book *Jews of Springfield in the Ozarks* (part of Arcadia Press' Images of America series), which documents the history of Springfield, Missouri's Temple Israel community pre-1960

- Multiple academic conference presentations by each of the lead researchers over the ten years.

The work was not completed by the two scholars alone. In fact, the majority of interviewing was accomplished by MSU service learning students during the *Seeing Traditions* portion of the project. This is not the least of three factors which make the *Telling Traditions/Seeing Traditions* project unique. The others include the fact that the Temple Israel Jewish community has been part of the Ozarks for more than 100 years and that the Ozarks region's population lacks diversity. The major lessons derived from ten years of experience are directly related to these facts.

Not surprisingly, repeated responses to products created for public programming consumption like the *Seeing Traditions* photographic exhibit and the project's documentary indicated not only that Missouri State Students and natives of the Ozarks had much to learn about a cultural group which had long been part of the region (ex. the photo of a Coke bottle on a Passover table below), but also that members of the larger Jewish community in the Ozarks, in Missouri, and in the South frequently had no idea of this long-time community, and no interest in helping preserve its history.

In point of fact, at the conclusion of the ten-year project, inquiries were made to archives —to St. Louis Jewish Community Archives (the largest in Missouri), and to Jewish archives for the Midwest and the South, to no avail. Each indicated the Ozarks region fell outside of their purview. Neither archive would take our project documents in their entirety. Rather, the director of each archive suggested discussion be taken up with the other or that we divide our documents according to the state they were collected in and donate them accordingly.

Ultimately as researchers, this meant we found that when the project ended it had really only just begun, for the Ozarks was a neglected region and the ten-year documentation of its largest Jewish community was destined to sit in boxes in the offices of the lead-researchers—or we would have to undertake the task of creating a home for the collection. At this point the greatest benefit of our academic associations came to our assistance. After lengthy discussions and sharing of correspondence with the Jewish archives, who could have claimed the Ozarks region as part of their collection area, the Missouri State Archives took possession of the documentation, forming the Ozarks Jewish Archive (OJA), which is now part of the Ozarkania collections. We were thrilled with this result, as some of our research also included brief collection forays into other small Jewish communities of the Ozarks, in places like Fayetteville, Fort Smith, and Hot Springs, Arkansas; Joplin and Cape Girardeau, Missouri and Muskogee, Oklahoma.

The Ozarks and Community Composition

MSU is located in Springfield, Missouri–the region's largest (population 151,580) and the United States' fourth most homogenous city, with a 91.7% white population in 2000 (U.S. Census 2000). The region is also known as the "buckle" of the Bible Belt, due to its heavily evangelical, Protestant population. Barring recent population changes in three of the western counties, where there has been an immigration of Latino populations since the 1990s, the homogeneity of Springfield is indicative not only of the regional population, but also that of the university, which though it tends—like most institutions of higher learning—to be both more liberal and more diverse than the surrounding region, has only 6% of freshman identifying as minorities (FA2003). Enrollment numbers for entering freshmen serve as a good representation of the overall student body. In the fall of 2003 at the beginning of this project, the student body numbered over 19,000. The freshman class of 2,668 individuals was composed of Missourians at the rate 92.3%, and slightly over one-third of those students (31.4%) were from the 24 county, southwest Missouri region (MSU). Consequently, central to the project's success was acknowledging the difference between the worldviews of most students and Temple Israel members.

Members of Temple Israel compose the largest synagogue in the 93-county Ozarks region (Rafferty 1-3). Here in the southwestern corner of the state, a Jewish community has gathered and conducted a Hebrew school since 1893. Community membership has not been uneventful for the congregation, nor activities exclusionary. For instance as recently as February 2001, community cemetery markers were defaced with swastikas. The local paper ran six articles covering community response to this event, including the fact that over 300 people of various faiths gathered within 24 hours to aid in the restoration of the defaced grave sites. Such experiences reinforce not only the sometimes overt racism expressed by factions of the community, but also Temple Israel's healthy membership in the area's interfaith community.

Service Learning and Public Programming

This project's melding of academic approaches (applied classroom knowledge during the interview process and service learning activities) and the production of public programming (in particular the *Seeing Traditions* photographic installation) raises questions about the value of such a project to collaborating service-learning educators and students; "Was this public history project of benefit in the classroom?" And if so, "Which classrooms?" Additionally, "What were the challenges inherent in the successful completion of this collaboration?"

Several research and teaching challenges were the result of this unique collaboration. Educational outcomes directly related to the service-learning portion of this project entailed creating a training package for participating students (who conducted interviews with women of the Temple Israel in Springfield, MO) and the Telling Traditions web site (*http://ozarksstudies.-missouristate.edu/tellingtraditions/*). At Missouri State University the Citizenship and Service Learning (CASL) center's service-learning activities are currently designed to enable educators offering service learning opportunities to their students to either propose a specific community collaborator and project for their course or offer students a specific project while leaving the choice of community partner to the student. Students who participated in the *Telling Traditions/Seeing Traditions* project entered with not only a variety of educational backgrounds and interests, but also diverse responsibilities to their individual courses. Preliminary preparation by the researchers took these facts into consideration, which resulted first in our defining oral history in its broadest sense and, second, in the design of an extra-long, two-hour (CASL) training session.

Defining oral history meant considering the various courses from which our workers would arrive: Jewish Studies, Folklore, Film, Photo Journalism, Journalism, Anthropology, Religious Studies, Creative Writing, etc., and considering the media we wished to use to document both individual interviews and community activities. Consequently, student training focused on defining oral history as the collection of oral commentary, material culture, and communal events on audio and video tape, film, and in writing. We did not include collection of three-dimensional objects although we strongly suggested that they be documented on film and encouraged discussion of them in interviews. This definition freed the lead researchers to emphasize each student's particular strengths and interests, facilitating the project's outcomes mentioned earlier.

From the first, there was one key area of concern in the orientation process. As researchers guiding students in a collaborative process where their work would be used to meet multiple classroom objectives, there was the concern that both student and instructor foci would not necessarily coincide with our own. Such concerns were justified only in one instance, when students were trained in interviewing by their instructor and not required to attend the two-hour training session. In this instance both students and their instructor were not prepared to make cold calls, and were surprised by community members' refusal to interview during high holy days. This first student experience highlighted the need for cultural training in conjunction with interview training, which would supplement training received from educators.

In the two-hour cultural-interview training sessions offered in subsequent semesters, emphasis was placed on orientation to the project and review of interviewing skills. Several handouts beyond those required for ethical interviewing (biographical form, interview questions, and release forms) were prepared, since students often chose to participate in order to learn basic skills. Additional forms included: a vocabulary sheet, a phone script, and an interview introduction script to facilitate students' need to navigate the preliminary interview process of making contact with a stranger and setting a time to meet (Appendix A).Though a list of prepared questions was available for students, they were advised to use questions as a guide and not read the page verbatim. Jewish culture was briefly introduced through handouts covering the main holidays and Hebrew terms frequently used in the community. During each of these and subsequent stages of the orientation process Margaret Yocom's list of techniques fieldworkers should use were emphasized (256-73).

Finally students were encouraged to observe their surroundings and note things that they did not recognize. This activity was encouraged for two reasons: to introduce the reason for cameras to be used in conjunction with taped interviews, and to inculcate the maxim that "respondents are the experts." Thus, we hoped to instill that the key to interviewing in an oral history project is listening to the individual being interviewed, learning from them, and asking about words, concepts, and household items in view that are unfamiliar. Students took this to heart and community members welcomed the chance to share their culture and their personal views, while teaching the willing. Consequently much student success in the area of cultural skill acquisition was due to face-to-face interaction with community members following the training sessions. And the combined efforts of researchers, community members and educators resulted in the majority of students attaining higher levels of cultural adjustment skills.

Cultural Adjustment Skills, a beginning point

Sending students to collect oral history from one of the Ozarks region's long-term minority groups presented several challenges. Questionnaire responses received at the end of each semester validated this assumption, as students openly discussed their knowledge of the local Jewish community. Overwhelmingly, responses were expressed in terms of stereotypical statements, suggesting that Jews were either "hidden," "just like me," or just like me "with old people speaking Hebrew." Such responses vividly highlight students' lack of intercultural knowledge.

We found that bringing students with—all too frequently—little multicultural experience and a strong acceptance of Christian proselytizing into direct contact with a culture differing from their own created for us a position of unique responsibility which shared certain characteristics commonly faced by the English as a Second Language (ESL) instructor. In both instances, students need to be introduced to new, unfamiliar cultures and cultural groups; thus, paradigms for cultural acquisition useful to ESL found application in our own work. In particular, the four stages of cultural awareness used by the University of Saskatchewan's TESOL certificate program (Module 6) allowed us to track students' growth in cultural acquisition skills and cultural understanding. The cultural awareness stages are:

Stage 1, individuals recognize the existence and influence of their cultural group and the existence of other cultures;

Stage 2, individuals attach value judgments to the perceived similarities and differences between their primary culture and American culture;

Stage 3, individuals choose to either solidify a monocultural view and retain an ethnocentric cultural perspective, or begin to think and act bi-culturally and create an integrated cultural perspective; and

Stage 4, individuals are able to: value and appreciate their own cultural roots, as well as other cultures; to see the strengths and weaknesses of any culture; and, to search for universals while valuing the diversity of the earth's cultures.

According to questionnaire responses recording students' beliefs about Jewish culture in the Ozarks, a select few began at Stage 3 of this cultural awareness paradigm, but nearly all began the project at Stage 1—even when they came from larger cities (e.g., St. Louis and Kansas City) with much larger Jewish populations or from a Jewish background.

In Stage 1, cultural recognition is often based on stereotypes or acknowledgement of obvious cultural or group identifiers, such as varying language, or differing dress and grooming traditions. Fifty percent of the students responding to questionnaires were at this stage and professed their knowledge of Ozarks Jewish community by indicating why they became part of the project with comments such as: "I thought the project would be interesting because I didn't know a whole lot about the Jewish culture;" by admitting such thoughts had not been important to them before the project, "I had not given it much thought, but with old people speaking in Hebrew;" or by emphasizing their lack of knowledge, "I didn't really know anything about the community before the project, but knew that it wasn't a large religion in the Ozarks" (Anon. St. Louis).

All students entering the project at Stage 3 had attained the second level of cultural acquisition skills. In Stage 2, individuals attach value judgments to the perceived similarities and differences between their primary culture and American culture. These students were primarily, though not all, from Jewish backgrounds in the larger metropolitan areas of St. Louis and Kansas City. Generally, their perspective transcended Stage 1 understanding due to having belonged to a minority cultural group in their home towns and having identified differences between their cultural and religious heritage and mainstream American culture.

Stage 3 is the point at which one chooses to either solidify a monocultural view and retain an ethnocentric cultural perspective, or begin to think and act bi-culturally and create an integrated cultural perspective. At the beginning of the project, students predominately presented two perspectives. One emphasized Temple Israel's religious isolation in the Bible Belt through comments such as, "At the beginning, I perceived Temple Israel as very small and hidden" (Jewish student from St. Louis/Kansas City) and I saw them "as a private rather secretive community of people who share a like religion and history" (Harlan). The other focused not on characteristics of the Ozarks region, but of Temple Israel itself. These students had read about the community in the local paper or met members of the community through school presentations. They had come to form opinions like that of one young man, who said, "I didn't know a whole lot about them. Rabbi Rita Sherwin once gave a talk to my High School English class, and I thought it was pretty progressive that they had a woman Rabbi" (Miles).

As researcher-educators in the areas of folklore and Jewish studies, Mara Cohen Ioannides and I aspired to offer students a learning environment that would inculcate a sense of the importance of oral history across diverse disciplinary perspectives, while fostering growth in the area of cultural adjustment skills. Ideally, we hoped, growth to at least the third stage in the cultural adjustment paradigm would occur, with a preponderance of students attaining this stage's integrated cultural perspective. However, project parameters regarding project training and implementation allowed little time for mentoring of students in cultural differences and acquisition skills even given the extra-long two-hour training session we negotiated for our project.

Teaching Interviewing: Where is the classroom? Who is the teacher?

As research coordinators, we were informal instructors for our student participants. The responsibility of preparing them to enter a new culture and of training them in interviewing techniques was formally ours for only two hours. Additional informal training occurred throughout the semester in one-on-one meetings at student request. Thus, one of the greatest challenges of this project was the brevity of our negotiated project orientation. As researchers guiding students in a collaborative process where their work would be used to meet multiple classroom objectives, we were also concerned that student and instructor foci would not necessarily coincide with our own. Consequently much student success in the area of cultural skill acquisition was due to the educational efforts of community members. The combined efforts of researchers, community members and educators resulted in the majority of students attaining higher levels of cultural adjustment skills.

Project Results, participating students

According to student surveys, both the two-hour orientation and the project resulted in positive learning experiences in the areas of culture and oral history. The majority of students completing the semester's interviewing project indicated they had learned a great deal about not only Judaism, but also culture, as they reached either Stage 3 or Stage 4 by the project's conclusion.

The Stage 3 students predominately focused on universals, describing community members as this young man did: "[they are] people just like me, with different backgrounds, customs, and religious ideas—but the same as anyone else basically" (Oveida). Such comments indicate a monocultural point of view that did not highlight or value the cultural differences he glosses over, by emphasizing "everyone's similarity."

In Stage 4, transcendence, students found that they were able to value and appreciate their own cultural roots, as well as other cultures, and to see the "individual strengths and weaknesses of any culture, and search for universals while valuing the vitality and variety of the earth's cultures" (*TESL* 1995: Module 6). Students who attained this level of cultural adjustment skills mentioned learning that Judaism "can be practiced in different ways, and means different things to those who do practice [it];" and that Judaism "is more than a religion, but a culture and/or lifestyle–it is much more encompassing than other religions in terms of how a life is lived. Judaism is the religion not a nationality. Judaism is practiced in their home as well as in their Temple" (Fansler). Others focused their comments jointly on the community and its religion, saying they learned that "[Temple Israel is] an interesting community and the members seem to be really close to one another; it's *another type* [student's emphasis] of group and they do many of the things the same way as many other religions" (Kopp). Each of these Stage 4 examples highlights in some way the community's similarities to and differences from the students' life experiences.

In the area of oral history, students were not only able to recognize the importance of collecting histories of various religious and ethnic cultures, but also to appreciate their discipline's role in the oral history collection process. Particularly edifying in this area were responses from students who were used to working in the media of video and film. Michael, a twenty-year old photography student, grappled with stating this mental shift when asked, "What did you learn about your field and oral history?" He responded,

Oral history is handed down verbally from generation to gen-

eration. If it's written down, then it's literate history. ... I
suppose maybe that, like oral history, pictures can be handed
down from generation to generation; [but] they're something
to be coupled with oral history, otherwise they're in danger of
becoming out of context. (Shadwell)

Clearly, working in a new environment and using new research techniques
allowed students an unparalleled learning opportunity in the areas of interviewing, cultural interaction, and cross-disciplinary knowledge application, as well as meaningful and representative primary research which
informed and buttressed much of the work the lead researchers produced
in subsequent years, on the web, in academic publications, and in the documentary format.

Ultimately, though extremely time consuming, the process of including
young scholars in the research process provided great dividends for both
students and lead researchers. The greatest was the time-consuming and
ever-present need to define, explain, and interpret the interview process
for these fledgling researchers; for the very act of interpreting folklore research approaches and products to a student audience with diverse scholarly backgrounds affords lead researchers the opportunity to re-envisage
their own research activities and products through multiple varied research lenses brought to the project not only by researchers, but also by
students, from different fields of academic study.

The most widely publicized product of this research process has been
the photograph exhibit, *Seeing Traditions* (ST). Envisioned as a display of
everyday Jewish life in the Ozarks, ST also existed to show people that
even though Judaism is different from the region's dominant Christian
religion, the people practicing Judaism are the same.[1] Based on visitors'
anonymous comments leaving the exhibit these goals were attained. As
one visitor commented: "I enjoyed the exhibit. I thought it was something
different, for it was unlike anything I have ever seen ... there were pictures
of normal everyday people. They weren't like the pictures ... in museums
of famous people." Yet, for ST to achieve this outcome, much behind the
scenes debate occurred.

The exhibit's process of creation and design was as much a learning experience for the researchers as the interview process was for students. Predominately learning arose while determining which photos should be included in the display. Central to discussions between the lead researchers

---

[1]During the time the exhibit was displayed, there were 78,022 visits to the library (Dur-
den); the majority of these had to pass by the photographs because of their central location
in the library.

was the fact that each was focusing on the need to present an under-represented community accurately. Obfuscating the process was the two researchers' three approaches towards clearly representing the community. First and foremost, the Jewish community should be represented in a manner accurate to the community's perception of itself. Second, Cohen's emphasis on Jewish Studies added an emphasis on historical accuracy. Third, Gholson desired to maintain an emphasis throughout the study on Jewish folklife. These approaches did not always value the same aspects of the community. Consequently, there were tense discussions on several key points. Two such discussions centered on specific photos, which were included in the exhibit.

This first photograph, of the Coke bottle on the community Passover dinner table, caused a heated argument. Cohen did not see anything interesting in this photograph. Gholson was pleased by the inclusion of the Coke bottle at a ceremonial dinner, a community Passover gathering. Cohen's response was "So? What's so important about a Coke bottle?" Gholson, "That right there. You prove the setting is all American by thinking it is not important, and your not recognizing the soda bottle as important means non-Jews will see this Coke bottle as very important because the bottle is a literal link between their culture and yours. The Coke bottle is popular American culture shared between American sub-cultures. The item will serve as a bridge connecting the viewer's American life experience to the American experience had by Temple Israel members." Incidentally, this greatly contested image was commented on the most by our audience. One anonymous Jewish viewer wrote, "[Exhibit] commentaries, also, touched on the fact that Temple Israel has always been a blend of long-held traditions and beliefs with social and cultural trends. I think this concept is exemplified beautifully in the photograph that shows a Seder plate and matzo sitting beside an open

bottle of Coca-Cola."

The second challenge faced in the creation of ST was community aesthetics. We had a series of photographs of the ritual table settings for Passover. Gholson wanted to present the various ways community members set their tables, while Cohen argued a public display of an important religious ritual should be respectful, with elegant place settings. The idea of what is "beautiful" became fraught with emotion because of the fear of outsider perceptions.

However, as one viewer commented: "I think place settings and the way the table is set up for the holidays, rituals, and gatherings is often overlooked. We, as gentile [i.e., non-Jewish] Americans, don't see it [i.e., the ritual meal] as being important, especially when paper or plastic is used. For some reason, the use of paper and plastic tends to devalue the place setting in our eyes. But in this case, we should not allow the use of paper and plastic to devalue these place settings because the required ritual objects are included" (Anon.).

Similarly, discussion arose about the inclusion of homemade versus artist-created Seder plates. The Passover Seder plate is used only at Passover to hold six symbolic foods that are eaten or displayed at the ritual meal which is part of the Passover celebration. Each of the items has special significance in the retelling of the story of the exodus from Egypt.

Again, how these plates would be viewed and the ritual and community perceived by the outside community was a central concern. One photograph included a young girl holding a Seder plate she had created, before glazing. An exhibit viewer commented, "the girl was very human ... humanity is something that we share...But in her humanity was also found her heritage, for the Seder tray she had just crafted is the continuation of legacy spanning generations of Jews and provides her and her family with their unique cultural history" (Anon.). Thus, the ultimate point of the exhibition, to present the Jewish community as relatable for the average audience of the Ozarks region, succeeded, at least for some viewers.

This project was a learning experience for the lead researchers on many levels. Our understanding of how communities view themselves and are viewed by others has been expanded. For Cohen, this was a lesson in how little the larger community really knows about minority cultures (WE-FLA). Gholson discovered folklorists' understanding of what is important to study is rarely consciously recognized by others. Both have broadened their appreciation of interdisciplinary, cross-cultural, and multi-generational dialogue as an approach for educational outreach, and the *Seeing Traditions/Telling Traditions* research products have subsequently modelled this in educational, museum, on-line, and film venues.

In addition to these personal take-aways, there were several lessons learned regarding researching and presenting public programming in a university setting. In regards to the use of students on a project:

  • the service learning construct does not lend itself to providing adequate training for fledgling interviewers and so would not be recommended unless the students to be trained are either already familiar with the cultural group to be studied or all possess previous technical training in the area they will be working in i.e., photography, videography, interviewing and project planning:

- Interviews by students can result in the collection of meaningful community history with great direction (prompting them to ask about a particular story) but requires significant additional time and effort on the part of the lead-researcher

- providing students with enough direction in regards to how to solicit and what types of narratives to solicit may require a greater knowledge of the community than a lead-researcher might have, even with a community scholar involved

- time to review student work outside of course requirements for grading must be factored into the project plan. It requires a significant amount of time for the review of documents selected for specific projects.

- significant time slots will also have to be placed into the programming plan for when specific documents are pulled for specific projects as there will be a need for BOTH researcher and community scholar to review images and quotes used in such projects. Similarly to Lawless' reflexive ethnography approach, this allowed the lead-researchers, which included a community scholar, to contrast and discuss their interpretations of particular images and quotes (305-06).

An example of one such review discussion occurred surrounding an image pulled from the final *Seeing Tradition* exhibit choices after the researcher revealed that the beautiful picture of a young female community member was deliberately framed when shot so that the window cross pieces behind her formed a cross. The community scholar had not seen what could be interpreted as a cross. She had to be taken step-by-step through thinking about how her own community members might feel about said picture after she repeatedly dismissed the importance of the "hidden symbol" because she loved the picture (which was of her own child) so much. How-ever, after an over-night break in discussion for thought, the exquisite image was removed from consideration for inclusion in the exhibit.

- Finally, time should be allowed for community feedback in the fullest sense, as promoted by Lawless' reflexive ethnographic approach. For our project that meant community pre-viewing of the documentary followed by discussion time and an early showing of the Seeing Tra-ditions photography exhibit where we requested direct or written feedback, based on attendees' personal preference. These communi-cations and critiques were reviewed and changes or additions made to the exhibits where needed, though no formal publication directly addressed them (311).

Based upon these instances of learning about research with service learning students and a co-researcher community scholar, this researcher concludes: first, the best use of service learning is when upper level students who have had technical training in a specific collection/documenta-tion technique are brought into the project. This is a great help because one is not teaching both technical skills and the community traditions, but just introducing the students to the community. Second, co-researchers, like service learning students, are most helpful when coming to the project with formal interview training in addition to training as community schol-ar/co-researchers. Third, either the addition of service learning or a co-researcher or community member untrained in either oral history or folk-lore research will require significant additional energy and time, as addi-tional training and additional time for important ethical discussions will be required.

Consequently though the benefits in learning about culture and cul-tural presentation for both students and lead-researchers are numerous and the use of students greatly speeds up the research process, this re-searcher would not recommend using service learning students who are not part of one's own classes or who are not at least one semester into their degree area course work, for utilizing students more advanced in their programs should allow them to bring significantly honed skills to the project. Finally, academics should think long and hard about the time re-quired of such projects, as peers may have little to no knowledge of the effort and significant additional time required to create meaningful and ethical public programming publications.

In spite of these obstacles the inclusion of service-learning in the re-search portion of this project resulted in several successes beyond the in-troduction of students to an actual research project. Foremost, a little known community with a history spanning more than a hundred years in the Ozarks was documented in photography and video over an entire year. Secondly and not less important, the need for institutions of the Ozarks region to promote and preserve self-documentation of the region's inhabitants and history was reinforced. Ultimately, these two successes laid the groundwork for many of the outcomes listed on the first two pages of this article, which would never have been accomplished as quickly without the hard, quality work of service-learning students.

Works Cited

Anon. *Seeing Traditions Project Comment Book.* 2005.

Fansler, R. *Telling Traditions, Service Learning Questionnaire.* January 18, 2004.

Cohen, Mara and M. Rachel Gholson. *Seeing Traditions.* Meyer Library, Missouri State University. Photographic Exhibit. 2005.

———. *Telling Traditions.* Ozarks Studies Institute. Missouri State. University. 2 September 2005. Web. 23 May 2016.
    < *http://ozarksstudies.missouristate.edu/tellingtraditions/* >.

———. *Issues in Communication and Culture: Research Design, Implementation, and Presentation of a Jewish Minority Culture in the American Midwest.* Published Conference Proceedings. WEFLA/Canadian Studies Conference. Holguín, Cuba: Universidad de Holguín, 2012 Web.

———. *Jews of Springfield in the Ozarks.* Images of America Series. Mt. Pleasant, SC: Arcadia P, 2013.

———. *Folklore, Service Learning, and the Documentary Process.* American Folklore Society, October 2005.

Harlan, R. *Telling Traditions, Service Learning Questionnaire.* January 18, 2004.

Keyes, Robert. "Six Teens Quizzed in Cemetery Vandalism." February 20, 2001. *Springfield News-Leader.* September 16, 2004.
    < *http://www.springfieldnews- leader.com/today/index.shtml* >.

Kopp, L. *Telling Traditions, Service Learning Questionnaire.* January 20, 2004.

———. "Nazi Symbols Painted on Gravestones." February 7, 2001. *Springfield News-Leader.* September 16, 2004.
    < *http://www.springfieldnews-leader.com/today/index.shtml* >.

Lawless, Elaine J. "'I Was Afraid Someone like You ... an Outsider ... Would Misunderstand': Negotiating Interpretive Differences between Ethnographers and Subjects." *The Journal of American Folklore* 105.417 (1992): 302-314

Miles, J. *Telling Traditions, Service Learning Questionnaire.* January 10, 2004.

Missouri State University. *Profile of First-Time Freshman, Fall 2003 Semester.* August 24, 2004. Office of Admissions. September 16, 2004. < *http://www.msu.edu/admissions/FFProfile.htm* >.

"Our View." February 7, 2001. *Springfield News-Leader.* September 16, 2004. < *http://www.springfieldnews-leader.com/today/index.shtml* >.

Oveida, E. *Telling Traditions, Service Learning Questionnaire.* January 20, 2004.

Rafferty, Milt. *The Ozarks: Land and Life.* 2nd ed. University of Arizona Press, Fayetteville, 2001.

Shadwell, Michael. *Telling Traditions, Service Learning Questionnaire.* January 15, 2004.

Strait, Jefferson. "Vandalized Cemetery Starts Over." February 12, 2001 *Springfield News-Leader.* September 16, 2004. < *http://www.springfieldnews-leader.com/today/index.shtml* >.

University of Saskatchewan. *TESL 31TESL Theory and Skills Development.* Certificate in Teaching English as a Second Language. Module 6. Saskatoon, Saskatchewan. 1995.

Wilson, Angela. "Cemetery to Be Rededicated." February 8, 2001. *Springfield News-Leader.* September 16, 2004. < *http://www.springfieldnews- leader.com/today/index.shtml* >

Yocom, Margaret R. "Family Folklore and Oral History Interviews: Strategies for Introducing a Project to One's Own Relatives." *Western Folklore* 41 (1982): 251-74.

Appendix A: Training and Interview Forms

Telling Traditions: An Oral History of the Women of Temple Israel
INSTRUCTIONS FOR STUDENTS

CONTACT'S: name
COMPLETE AND FORWARD TO US:

- student information forms (now)
- the National Institute of Health (NIH) — Protection of Human Research Subjects course certificate. This can be located at: *http://cme.-cancer.gov/cgibin/cms/cmspartr5.pl?option=3* or through the Office of Sponsored Research website. Send us a hard copy of the certificate of completion. **Without this certificate you CANNOT participate!**

INTERVIEW PROCESS:

39616. You will be assigned people to contact and arrange an interview with. We will send you their name and phone number.

39617. Go to Blackboard and print out a phone dialogue sheet before you call to arrange an interview.

39618. Call the Media Services Equipment in Meyer Library (x65778) and reserve a tape recorder and digital camera (you'll need a disk for it) for the day you need it. Make sure to tell them you are participating in Telling Traditions.

39619. Go to Pummill Hall Room 205 and collect (if it isn't open, see one of us):

- 1 green folder with 2 release forms, 1 biography form, 1 packet of questions (these items are available on Blackboard)
- at least 2 audio tapes and 1 disposable camera (if no digital cameras are available)
  Make sure you sign out the tapes, camera, and folder in the green binder.

5. Interview process:

- review the release form with the subject and both of you sign it
- fill in the biography form
- conduct the interview
- take about 2 photos of the subject
- offer the subject 1 copy of the release form

6. Return the tape recorder and camera to Media Services Equipment.

7. Follow the instructions for a tape log (also found on Blackboard) of the interview:

39784. E-mail one of us. Don't forget to include the person's name.

9. Return to Pummil Hall Room 205 to the appropriate boxes:
   - green folder with 1 release form, 1 bio form, 1 packet of questions, 1 tape log
   - used audio tapes, blank audio tapes, and the disposable camera to appropriate box. Sign in camera, tapes, and folder.

10. Email us the transcription and the photo from the digital camera (or the disposable camera number and photo number) and notification of completion (including the number of hours more you need for credit).

Each interview will take between 1 and 2 hours.

Instructions for the Interview

What is the Accession number?

It is a reference code used by the researcher to make sure that anonymity is maintained in the study. It is usually designed by the researcher.

How do I make an Accession number?

It begins with the date of the interview in the following order: the last two digits of the year, two digits for the month, two digits for the day. There is no separation or punctuation between the pairs of numbers. Add to the end of number the subject's first and last initial. For example, an interview of Miriam Wise on July 5, 2002 would have the accession number of 020705MW. If this is still confusing, leave it off of the paper work and we'll take care of it.

The interview:

1. Make sure the tape recorder is working.

2. Review the "Release of Rights Form" with the respondent.

3. Both of you need to complete and sign both copies.

4. You need to ask the questions on the "Biographical Data Sheet" and fill it out. Do NOT give it directly to the respondent.

5. Turn on the tape recorder and ask the questions in the question packet. You need not ask questions that have been answered in the course of previous questions. Feel free to add your own questions. Remember: This is NOT about you. You should say VERY LITTLE other than to ask the questions and encourage the subject to answer. You should be polite at all times, answering any questions posed by the person being interviewed. If the question is of a personal nature or on a subject you are not comfortable with, be open and honest. Offer the information you are comfortable discussing and say you are not comfortable with the rest.

6. Thank the respondent when you are done.

7. Ask if they wish to change their preference for release on the "Release of Rights Form." Offer them a copy of the "Release of Rights Form."

8. Collect your papers, notes, and tape recorder.

Missouri State University
901 South National, Springfield, MO 65804
Telling Traditions: **Biographical Data Sheet**

Accession number _____

Place of interview _____   Date(s) of interview _____

_____

****

Collectors are requested to get as possible of the data below on each person interviewed/ recorded, either from conversation or direct query. Full background information adds historical value to the interview or recording.

Name _____

        PRINT in Block letters: LAST NAME, First Name, (Maiden Name) etc. and how referred to

locally.

Place of birth _____

Community lived in during first 5-10 years _____

Places of residence (including significant travel) with years _____

_____

Age _____   Date of Birth_____

Education _____

_____

Occupation(s) Past and Present _____

Father's (full) name

_____

Birth place of FATHER and place of residence (with years if possible) _____

Grandfather lived where? _____

_____   Grandmother lived where?_____

_____

When and from where did ancestors originally come to the Ozarks? _____

_____To the U.S.? _____

_____

Religion _____ Any changes? _____

_____

Mother's (full) name _____

(maiden)_____

Birth place of MOTHER and place of residence (with years if possible) _____

_____

_____

Grandfather lived where? _____

_____

Grandmother lived where?_____

When and from where did ancestors originally come to the Ozarks?_____

_____ To the U.S.? _____

_____

Release of Rights Form
Telling Traditions Interview Project

Accession number _____

You are invited to participate in an interview project conducted by M. Rachel Gholson and Mara W. Cohen Ioannides (English Department). If you decide to participate, the student and/or instructor will be conducting a tape recorded, oral history interview concerning your life history or family history, experiences, traditions, and reflections. The interview will be between thirty minutes and two hours in length. The interviewer may request a follow-up interview at a later date. The interview will be recorded and photos taken with your permission. You may withdraw at any time from participation in this project. Since we are tape recording this interview, we may record statements you make about yourself or others that you may not want to have included in the public archive. In order to minimize this risk, you will be asked to sign a release form only at the end of the interview, so that you will be fully aware of the content of the interview before agreeing to or restricting its public use and preservation. Participation is voluntary; your refusal to participate will involve no penalty to either the subject or the student researcher, and you may discontinue participation at any time.

You may stipulate below any restrictions on and conditions for the use of the tape recording or other collected materials and information including publication and preservation. You may also stipulate that you must review a tape copy or transcript before the material is placed in an archive; you may place restrictions on the public use of portions of these materials at that time. If you do not stipulate restrictions, the recording may be donated to a public archive and the data collected may be used for research, publications, exhibits, course materials, or multi-media productions. With your approval below, student projects may be "published" on a world wide web page.

Thank you for your cooperation. You will receive a copy of this form for your records. If you have any questions now or additional questions later, we will be happy to answer them. Feel free to contact the supervising faculty member, Rachel Gholson, English Department, Missouri State University, 901 South National, Springfield, MO 65804, 417-836-5180. I agree to participate in the interview project described above. I understand that I may withdraw from this project at any time. Initial here to indicate you've read the information above. _____

I hearby give permission for any lawful public use including publication of the recording and information collected except for the following conditions:

__ no restrictions;__ for research use only, not to be archived;

__ for use with the following restrictions:_____

__ I would like to review a tape copy or transcript before it is placed in an archive.

Signature of Interviewee:_____

Signature of Legal Guardian (for interviewees under 18): _____

Name (please print): _____ Date:___/___/___

Address and Phone Number: _____

_____ (___)____-_____

Signature of **Narrator**:_____

Name (please print)_____ Date:___/___/___

Address and Phone Number:_____

_____ _____

Phone Dialogue Sheet

Hello,
May I speak with Mr./Mrs./Ms. (respondent's full name)?
If not available, leave a message and make sure to include the following information.

- Who called: **Telling Traditions**
- When you can be contacted: day and best times
- Your phone number

Hi, I'm (your name) from the SMSU Telling Traditions project that was announced in the Temple's June newsletter. Are you familiar with the project?
If so:

> Are you interested in participating? Great then, I would like to make an appointment to interview you for the project.

If not:

> Would you like to learn more about the project and it's goals?
>
> Telling Traditions is a project that documents how Judaism is part of the daily life of Springfield women. We are interested in talking to all female members of the congregation in the area. It's important to document women who are cantors or rabbis, but it is equally important to learn how Judaism is part of the lives of every woman. (Daily activities performed by women who cook in the home, help prepare and organize holiday celebrations, and are mothers teaching religion and its tradition to their children tell us much about synagogue life.)
>
> Telling Traditions' three main goals are:
>
> - to learn about the breadth of temple members' experiences in Springfield and the Ozarks;
> - to learn about food and food traditions in the community and the community's families; and
> - to understand how women learn about and choose the many roles they fill in the community.
>
> Do you have any questions about the project for me?
>
> Does this sound like a project you would be willing to participate in?

If so:

Great then, I would like to make an appointment to interview you for the project.

If not:

May I ask why you are not interested? (Write the answer down, even if the answer is "no you may not", so you can turn it in.)

Thank you for your time, (Mr./Ms. Last name)! Goodbye.

Appendix B: Glossary of Jewish Words and Questions

Cantor: a religious leader of the Jewish community trained in music.

Conservative: a middle of the road Jewish sect, which tries to maintain traditional practices in a modern world.

Hannukah: an eight day festival that falls in the winter. It celebrates the victory of the Macabees (a Jewish guerilla army) around 150 BCE over the Greeks, who destroyed the Temple in Jerusalem. While many associate it with Christmas, its importance in the Jewish calendar is relatively minor. Traditionally, candles are lit, fried foods eaten, and coins or gifts exchanged.

Havdalah: the closing ceremony of the Sabbath, which reminds the Jew that a holy period has ended. It is marked with the blessing of a special candle, wine, and spices.

High Holy Days: beginning with Rosh Hashanah and ending with Yom Kippur. It happens in the fall in Sept or Oct, depending on the Jewish calendar which is lunar. The holiest time on the Jewish calendar when Jews reflect on the previous year and purify themselves for the next one. Some believe that this is the time when G-d decides who will live through the year.

Jew: a person who is monotheistic and follows the practices of Judaism. They do not believe that Jesus is the Messiah. They are awaiting the arrival of the Messiah.

Jewish: when used in reference to a language, it means either Hebrew (though most people use the word Hebrew) or more likely Yiddish

Jewish week: begins on Sunday and ends on Saturday when the first star appears in the sky.

Jewish year: based on a lunar calendar where the months have twenty-nine or thirty days (there is a leap month to adjust the calendar). The year is 354 days long. Beginning the evening of Sept. 7, 2002 is the year 5762. The years are counted according to when the great rabbis believed the beginning of the world was, using the story in Genesis as the basis.

Kashrut: see kosher

Kosher: laws pertaining to food. There are dictates about what can be eaten: no shellfish, pork, or carnivores; only birds, scaled fish, and cud-eating, split-hooved creatures. One cannot eat meat and dairy at the same meal. There are numerous rules about slaughter and keeping of food, dishes, and kitchens.

Orthodox: the most traditional of the Jewish sects. They follow the letter of the law. Men and women have separate roles in the community.

Passover: an eight day festival in the spring commemorating the Exodus from ancient Egypt. During this time, Jewish individuals may not eat any foods with leavening agents (yeast, baking soda, etc.) this includes: bread, cake, cookies, pasta.

Pesach: see Passover

Rabbi: a religious leader of the Jewish community. The word means teacher, they are not a holy person.

Reconstruction: a liberal Jewish sect, which has reinterpreted some of the laws.

Reform: the most liberal of the Jewish sects. They follow the meaning of the laws. Men and women do not have different roles in the community.

Rosh Hashanah: the New Year on the Jewish calendar which occurs during the fall.

Sabbath: a holy day and the seventh day of the week, Saturday, a day of rest. It begins Friday night at sundown and continues until Saturday at sundown. At home, the opening of the holiday is marked by the blessing of candles, wine, and bread; the closing is marked by Havdalah. During Sabbath, no work may be done except that needed for survival. Thus there is no cooking, cleaning, using of lights, driving of a car, etc. in the Orthodox tradition.

Seder: the ceremonial meal on the first and second night of Passover during which the story of the Exodus is retold. This festival takes place in the spring.

Shabbat/Shabbas: see Sabbath

Shul: see synagogue

Synagogue: the building in which Jews pray and study. The Hebrew term includes three concepts: house of prayer, house of study, and house of community.

Temple: see synagogue

Yiddish: spoken by Jews of East European descent, a form of middle German written with Hebrew characters

Yom Kippur: the White Fast, the last day of the Holy Days.

Questions

Where were you raised?

Were you a child-member of a synagogue or religious congregation? What kind?

What is it that you view/feel makes you Jewish?

Are there other ways to be Jewish? If so, what are they?

When did you join Temple Israel and how old were you?

If you joined as an adult, why did you?

How would you describe your membership in the Temple? (only prompt if necessary: What adjective would you use to describe your membership: active, interested, transient, collegial, etc.)?

Who or what has been the greatest influence on your being Jewish and why?

In general, who or what do you see as a major influence in preserving Judaism?

In this congregation, who do you see as a major influence in preserving Judaism?

What specific activities do you participate in with the congregation? Why these activities?

Do you or have you had a leadership role in the congregation? Why did you do it?

Have you acted as a mentor to other women (those over 13) in the congregation? How? Why? (If not already answered.)

Do you see some activities as more vital to preserving Judaism than others? Which and why?

How do you practice Judaism? (only prompt if necessary: For example, celebrating the holidays, keeping kosher, going to services, participating in the synagogue social life)

Do you feel that women have a special role in Judaism? What is it?

What Jewish women have shaped you as a Jewish woman and how? (only prompt if necessary: Have there been any outside/inside your family?)

What Jewish men have shaped you as a Jewish woman and how? (only prompt if necessary: Have there been any outside/inside your family?)

Do you take responsibility for certain celebrations or preparations for religious holidays?

Which ones?

Repeat for each activity, as necessary:

How did you become involved?

Who helps? (only prompt if necessary: ages, genders, etc.)

Have these been part of synagogue life for a long time?

Who would traditionally plan and create these events in the past?

How does home preparation/celebration differ from that of the synagogue? From other families in the community?

In your experience, do these participating individuals participate in other religious activities as a group? ... on their own?

Are there ways that you practice or teach Judaism/religion to your family members that differ from the ways your mother practiced or taught you?

How did your mother's role differ from your father's?

To your knowledge was your mother's approach to Judaism/religion different from the approach of your mother-in-law's? If so, how?

Are there family celebrations (or parts of celebrations) that have a religious element and are not celebrated at the synagogue (elements of birthdays, anniversaries, etc.?)

Do you feel it is the role of the synagogue, the family, both or neither to educate children in the traditions of Judaism? If it is the family, which member of the family takes the dominant role?

How does the family play a role, if it does?

(The indented questions are only for those women with children.)

Do you teach Judaism in your home to your children?

If so, how? (by example, planned lessons, supplemental talks)

(couples)

Do you have a role that differs from your husband's in educating the children?

If so, how?

If you have children of both genders, do they take responsibility for roles in family celebrations of a religious nature? What are these? Are they different for your boys and girls? If so, how?

Is this different from what you experienced as a child? How?

Are there activities or ways you mark your belief that are traditional (passed from parent to child)?

What are some examples of these?

Does the synagogue also mark these elements of the Jewish faith?

If so, how are your family's traditional activities different from formal synagogue activities?

Food

Are there foods or recipes that you feel are traditionally Jewish?

Why are these Jewish foods and not American, for example?

Are these foods ever shared with people from outside the community? When and how?

Is it ever difficult to find ingredients for traditional recipes in Springfield?

Where can you find Jewish food items in town?

If you cannot find certain items, do you adjust the recipes or bring the items in from elsewhere?

If from elsewhere, how do you find the items and where do they come from?

Do you ever adapt standard American or other ethnic dishes so that they are Jewish? Which ones? How do you adapt them? When do you eat these dishes? With whom?

Can you think of other roles Jewish women take that we have not discussed here?

Is there anything else you want to add?

Ozark River Storytelling: Social Networks, Narrative, and Courtship in a Modern Rural Festival (Mariah Marsden)

On March 26 of 2016—Easter weekend—over twenty La Russell, Missouri neighbors and friends filtered in and out of the first Ozark River Storytelling event. The steady waters of Spring River tossed sunlight all day long, and the river was full on the bank from the rain the day before. The area lies at the foot of a bluff that cuts through the river bottoms, hayfields, and patches of brushy woods. To the north of the campsite lies a stream that flows from the woods, which visitors must cross in order to reach the riverside. Not every vehicle can make this trek. Spring River runs south of the site, east to west, from the old, long-gone city of Bowers Mill to the larger city of Carthage which lies almost thirty miles downstream. This waterway is popular with canoers. The storytelling event took place on this Marsden campsite, which has long been the site of social gatherings and barbeques. Fish and potatoes were cooked in a fryer. Camping chairs were moved around as the sun moved overhead. A guitar was tuned, and someone sang about rotten love and fiery marriages.

Far too often, writers and academic scholars interested in exploring the folklife of the Missouri Ozark region portray this folklife as an endangered (if not already extinct) culture, treating the vernacular traditions—the gristmills, the shivaries, the yarb doctors and the water diviners, old superstitions and settler folk stories—as historic artifacts that are irrevocably compromised by the intrusion of popular culture into once-isolated areas. In her 1992 publication of *A Living History of the Ozarks*, Phyllis Rossiter echoes this nostalgic worry:

> The old ways and the old ideas are slipping away. Forests are being bulldozed, hills leveled to facilitate better bridge approaches, roads straightened and widened to accommodate motor homes and boat trailers. Once known only by local names and left unmarked, unpaved country roads are now numbered and signed to ease the jobs of the latter-day paramedics and firemen. (32)

Here it is significant to note that the "old ways" and "old ideas" are invariably connected to the material life of the Ozarks: the roadways, the impassible hanging bridges, the informally named dirt roads. What does this mean for those areas of the Ozarks now connected by interstates, paved county roads, and airports? Without the insulating guard of isolation, what is to become of the local traditions that had been maintained and preserved from generation to generation? Writers like Rossiter respond to this anxiety, documenting and celebrating the old ways in an hard-bitten attempt to "safeguard [Ozark] history, its culture, its community memory, to keep it from being replaced by the *alternate histories* that regions sometimes erect for themselves when the real history is forgotten" (Rossiter 456, original emphasis). There is a strong preservationist bent in modern Ozark folklore studies. Many researchers and enthusiasts look backwards in time, isolating the distant Ozark traditions that seem exotic or removed from daily life. Granted, reflection is a worthwhile endeavor that pushes us to engage with our past. To limit our research to historic investigation, however, is to assume that traditional Ozark culture is removed from contemporary everyday life. Having spent most of my life living in the western corner of the Missouri Ozarks, I have found that not enough attention is paid the adapting, evolving, living folklore that exists and grows in the modern-day Ozark hills.

I have been collecting and studying the narratives and traditions of this area for almost a year. I have laughed with blue-collar wordsmiths and enjoyed the lively stories shared by cattlewomen. My father, Forrest Marsden, one of the well-known storytellers and tradition-bearers in the community, has facilitated and mediated these moments, introducing me to friends of the family and local characters with colorful reputations. When I approached my father about hosting a storytelling event for the locals, he was enthusiastic in his support. I developed a formal invitation for him to distribute freely amongst those community members he knew personally.[1] This flyer was the extent of my planning for the event. My father prepared the campsite at the access point; my mother, Catherine Marsden, prepared some of the food and procured the beverages; and the other participants brought their own river gear, food, and artifacts to share.

It is my ongoing goal to collect and celebrate the vibrant, adaptive folklife of this region, and to emphasize the living nature of Ozark folklore. Folklorists Martha C. Sims and Martine Stephens stress this living quality: "Folklore is lived, experienced, created, and shared by people" (31). In response to the preservationist imperative held by Rossiter and others, I am working to draw critical attention to the synthetic, imaginative, and hybridized traditions of places like my hometown of La Russell in the western corner of the Missouri Ozarks. While the foundations of many artifacts, customs, and stories are no longer active in the everyday lives of modern Ozarkers, public celebrations and community events facilitate the informal communicative practices of vernacular groups that function today, now, in the real world. However, the Ozark River Storytelling event— soon to be a biannual festival—is not merely an opportunity for scholars and enthusiasts to consider the direction of modern Ozark folklore studies. The event, while originally conceived as an opportunity for collection and fieldwork, has gained its own significance within local community. The unstructured nature of the first event gave participants the opportunity to shape the affair to suit their needs and interests. Roger Abrahams writes of this process in *Everyday Life: A Poetics of Vernacular Practices*: "We seek to merge our all-too-limited selves with some larger group of celebrants and to escape the constraints of our daily existence by plunging into the seemingly unbounded possibilities offered by theater, rituals, and festivals" (4). Through public display and performance, individuals can make sense of their experiences in a new and generative space. The participant response at the Ozark River Storytelling event—as stations, stories, artifacts, customs, and other lore all took shape in the moment—reveals the complex ways in which this social group navigates unstable, unstructured situations even as they work to make sense of their community experience, particularly when it comes to inter-family relations and courtship.

Here, I am interested in investigating the ways in which storytellers and raconteurs use their stories to manage dynamic social relationships in the midst of a festival. The Ozark River Storytelling event was a fluid, flexible situation that gave rise to certain vernacular elements that were not prefigured or calculated. I will consider the customary structures that developed during the event, paying particular attention to how the event

---

[1]See Figure 1 in the Appendix.

took on the form and structure of a festival. I will then explore and analyze a particular narrative shared at the event that further demonstrates the traditional ways in which social and familial bonds are negotiated, reinforced, and explicated. Ultimately, I hope to demonstrate how this modern social group uses tradition and traditional structures at an event to manage chaos on the material level (through formalized festival features) and the imaginative level (narratives and storytelling).

A Dynamic Social Network

The tiny town of La Russell lies just over forty-five miles west of Springfield, Missouri.[2] Straddling the boundary of Jasper and Lawrence Counties, the town proper consists of only a few municipal and commercial businesses: namely, Whitehead's Farm Supply store, the local post office branch, and Tom Garrison Logging & Lumber. The most important geographical feature is Spring River.[3] It has played a significant role in the development and social relations of the community over time. Bowers Mill, one of the early nineteenth-century townships in the area, was established after the Bowers family harnessed the power of the river for their milling operation, spurring commercial growth and interest in this location. Even after La Russell was established in 1904, local residents and neighbors would gather on Island No. 10, which was a five-acre stretch of land that formed when the river split and rejoined downstream. Participants called this event "Everybody's Picnic," and natives still remember the big bands and Easter pageants that went on by the riverside (Chrisman 81). Today, locals still make use of the area along Spring River as a gathering place.

The Everts clan. The Chrismans. The Proberts. Yahanna Garrison. The Marsden family. Jeff Wilks. Some of the Ozark River Storytelling participants had never met each other before the event in March of 2016. Rick Jones had gone on prospecting trips to North Carolina and Colorado with Forrest Marsden but had yet to be introduced to Forrest's neighbors, the Everts, whose land sat just across from the Spring River campsite. Robert

---

[2]The spelling of the city name has been contested for many years with variations from source to source. *The History of LaRussell* features various incarnations, including "Larussell," "La Russell," and the titular "LaRussell." I will be using the form more commonly used today, "La Russell," which is also featured on the city's signage.

[3]In a promotional pamphlet developed in the early twentieth century, the LaRussell Commercial Club describes the town's geographic location: "The town is beautifully located on a slightly [sic] elevation one-half mile south of Spring river, and by reason of its natural advantages in elevation and drainage, affords very desirable sites for business and residence purposes" (3).

"Bob" Alexander, a folksinger and friend of Rick Jones, had not met Larry and Debbie Chrisman, who often hunted (arrowheads and deer) on the Marsden property. I had yet to personally meet the majority of the visitors before that Easter weekend, but I had heard their stories from my father. Many were Forrest's personal friends, or men and women with whom he had done business, or area residents, or traveling companions, or casual acquaintances. Amidst this disparate group of people, Forrest became the tangible, living touchstone individuals used to position themselves in relation to each other, and their stories reflected some of this negotiation. Jeff Wilks, Forrest's childhood friend, offered teasing hints of their youthful escapades to those listeners looking for embarrassing stories about their host. Rick Jones regaled listeners with stories of their intrepid treasure-hunting adventures together in the Colorado Rockies. Larry Chrisman brought out his polished rock collection and talked about the time when Forrest had brought over some polished flint and introduced him to rock tumbling.[4] The Ozark River Storytelling event brought together people who shared common interests—arrowheads, local history, fishing, and gossip—but who had yet to gather as a group. The interrelationships of this social network were only just beginning to develop in concrete ways. Because of this, the shared values and interests of these individuals became symbols that confirmed the relationships between families, friends, and neighbors—old and new.

These shared interests were invoked in a number of material, tangible ways. Before guests arrived, my father stopped at the arrowhead field on the way down to the river campsite. A section of an old horse pasture on the hill, this ground has been aerated and scoured by Forrest for any trace of flint that had been shaped by native peoples: ancient drills, ceremonial tips, scrapers, bird points. Some of the participants of the Ozark River Storytelling event had visited this area before and had hunted for arrowheads with Forrest. When they entered the gate and headed towards the campsite that March afternoon, they were greeted by a sign at the field reading: NO ARROWHEAD / HUNTING OR POLITICAL SPEACHES [sic] / VIOLATORS PROSECUTED / UNDER PENALTY OF LAW.[5] It was a modified hunting restriction Forrest had posted as a kind of inside joke, to the obvious delight of participants. Many of them took pictures of the sign and immediately posted them to various social media. In actuality, the hunting sign meant quite the opposite to these participants; instead of forbidding arrowhead hunting, Forrest openly encouraged them to try their luck that day. The significance of this sign lay in the rules of permission

---

[4]See Figure 2 in the Appendix.
[5]See Figure 3 in the Appendix.

and acceptance: only those allowed by the landowner may search in the fields, and those participating in the storytelling event were offered this hospitality. Invitation immediately generates exclusivity, tightening the bonds between those in attendance and laying the foundation for more personalized relationships.

Community economics also played a role in how participants formed their social network. As hosts, Forrest and Catherine Marsden were in charge of choosing supplies. At Forrest's specific request, beer was purchased from the nearby Sarcoxie liquor store: a place he continues to support to make sure that it stays in business. Potato salad was ordered from the local Mennonites at the Circle E general store, which is known for its buttery pies and no-nonsense, sparely packaged food. Fresh, fried fish was prepared onsite, and it had been caught by Nate Everts and his son on a fishing trip the day before in Stockton Lake. Community connections were forged through the food, demonstrating not only general support for local businesses but also the performance of this support. Participants at the festival celebrated their connections to the area in a visible, tangible, savory way. The foodways of this group embody the economic connections within the community rather than recipe traditions that have been traditionally circulated amongst members.

As I reflect on the presentation and exchanges that took place on the banks of Spring River, I begin to see elements of public festival at play at the storytelling event: makeshift artifact stalls, impromptu stages, "redneck fireworks."[6] Little to no planning was done in preparation for the event beyond gathering food. The spontaneous development of musical performance and other formalized presentations show how participants navigated a new social scene and worked to develop a context-specific communal sensibility. By "communal sensibility," I mean that this group, together, developed a set of assumptions about what should be on display: what elements of their private lives should be broadcast or dramatized, and what information should be glossed over.

The Ozark River Storytelling communal sensibility developed not in a nebulous, abstract way, but through the spontaneous festival structure that began to take shape. In *Everyday Life*, Abrahams describes the nature of festivals and the ways in which ordinary people bring artistry and poetic measure to day-to-day living. He analyzes the material and symbolic elements of festivals, features which clarify and bring to light certain undercurrents within the group (155). Even as he breaks down the com-

---

[6]Nate Everts put on a display of these "redneck fireworks" at nightfall as the camping gear and food was being put away. He used an empty beer bottle, gas from his truck, and a perforated bottle cap to produce a good-sized flame that whistled as it flared out of the gasoline-filled bottle that rested above the fire on a grate.

ponents of everyday living, Abrahams articulates the negotiation of the public and private that takes place in community events (4). Individual sensibilities and "constraints" become secondary to the larger communal sense of aesthetics, civility, presentation, and purpose. This is not to say that the individual is subsumed into the community; the process is neither seamless nor smooth. Individuals must negotiate their public and private lives, and this often leads to tension and resistance, which did manifest in the Ozark River Storytelling event. But the spontaneous festival structure can be seen as a vernacular response to social instability—a mechanism which helps individuals from the community make sense of developing relationships, organize their narratives, and develop a context-specific sensibility. By analyzing the shape and structures that arose during this event, I can better understand the imaginative and material dimensions of this area: how individual groups form in these communities, how the public and the private are negotiated, and how narrative might work for and against social cohesion.

Visible, material markers—the arrowhead fields, signs, food, and riverside setting—build connections between participants at the festival, forming common points of personal and public experience even as these elements are attached to community values. The network of symbols and objects forms the foundation for the narratives shared in this space. These material touchstones create a sense of tradition that then informs the content and shape of the stories shared at the event. They provide the context that influences the storytelling performances and creates the playful, energetic atmosphere of a festival.

Significantly, the communal sensibility of the Ozark Storytelling event was also shaped by imaginative decisions: what stories were shared amongst the group, what values were emphasized, and what information was held back from group discussion. This process is context-specific because timing, place, and group members can also impact sensibility. Since it occurred over Easter weekend, extended relatives from the Everts family were visiting from Kentucky and eager to share embarrassing childhood memories. Participants made use of the open, outdoor space to set up smaller stations for festival activities that combined with storytelling circles. Anglers on Spring River told fishing stories; the meat preparation sparked hunting tales; rock displays on tailgates led to arrowhead hunting anecdotes. Again, the specific relationships and connections (or disconnections) between attendees determined appropriate story topics. For example, it was only after one couple left the event that a particularly ribald, bawdy story could be told—a tale that I will analyze below in order to show how storytellers navigate and build their social landscape at a public event.

Dirty Dishes and Vaseline: Interpreting Narrative

Of the stories shared and recorded at the Ozark River Storytelling event, there was one tale that particularly thrilled the audience even as it attracted my interpretive attention. As the sun dipped towards the western horizon that March day, the participants who had gathered to watch the corn-holing game began to demand more stories. Nate Everts, known for his ornery tales and storytelling skills, was called forward. The Everts women told him to "get up there," and he took center-stage in the zoysia grass, facing the audience in their camping chairs. "Nate!" one participant shouted. "The Motorcycle, Nate!" That title was all it took to get the Everts laughing and the other participants leaning forward with expectant attention. Nate Everts pulled up a chair, sighing dramatically as he said that it was going to be a long one (though it was actually a shortened version).[7]

The ensuing narrative was a sample of some of the best bawdy lore alive in the Ozarks today.[8] A close consideration of the thematic, symbolic, mimetic, and rhetorical elements of this narrative reveals the generative power of folklore and public storytelling: its capacity to shape and restructure social relations even as it cultivates a context-specific communal sensibility. As I analyze the text, context, and texture of Nate Everts's narrative, I will first consider the story elements and the Ozark storytelling traditions that have been adapted and incorporated into the performance. I will also consider the mimetic elements of the story: the raconteur's insistence that it is a personal narrative describing his own youthful dalliances with a family that was well-known to his audience. By parsing the rhetorical and imaginative triggers of this text, I will demonstrate how narratives function as a way of managing and solidifying specific social relations through the theme of courtship. Storytelling is a way of manufacturing a social structure that, in this example, worked alongside the structure of the storytelling festival as a way of bringing order to an unstable, chaotic situation.

In Everts's courtship narrative, an inexperienced young man wants to impress a girl by getting a motorcycle. He buys what is available: a faulty machine that has trouble functioning in the rain. However, he is told that if he rubs Vaseline on the fuel tank to wick away the water, all's well. The

---

[7]See Figure 7 in the Appendix.
[8]For a full transcription of "The Motorcycle," see the Appendix.

girl is suitably impressed by the motorcycle, and they make plans for a date. The boy learns he must pass a kind of test: dining with her folks in the family home. Out of his element, the suitor learns that there is a strange custom in this household. Whoever talks at dinner has to clean the dishes. In a house packed with greasy plates and moldy utensils, it is clear to the boy that no one has spoken in a very long time. Determined to win the challenge and win the girl, the boy focuses on the father and tries to spur him into talking. In a series of escalating dares, the boy seduces the girl at the dinner table as her father watches. The father stays silent in this battle of wills, so the young man moves up to the mother of the house. Again, the father says nothing. Suddenly, in the midst of his sexual play, the young man hears a clap of thunder and races over to get his Vaseline from his coat pocket at the table. Seeing the Vaseline, the father jumps up and forcefully declares, "I'll do dishes."

The narrative is told from the boy's point of view—more specifically Nate Everts's point of view. The first-person narration is flexible, moving from self-effacing commentary ("I wasn't very cool, and she liked cool guys") to the development of a trickster-voiced internal dialogue (*"I bet I know a way to get him to talk"*).[9] The narrative is, at its heart, about the transition from innocence to experience. After the girl agrees to go on a date with him, Everts declares: "Man I was excited. I'd been looking forward to that my whole life." The narrator is affable, easy-going, evidenced by his repeated answers to the unfolding scene at the dinner table. "Well alright," he says again and again as he learns of the odd quirks of the family and the challenge he must overcome. His initial passive acceptance of the dinnertime rules contrasts sharply with the active, aggressive scheme that unfolds as he faces off against the father at the dinner table.

The father-figure is the personified challenge to the narrator's transformation. "Dad" is the dramatic obstacle the suitor must overcome, and the paternal character is given attitude and form when Everts dramatically mimics the father's pose at key moments in the story. The contest comes to a head when the narrator recognizes that it is the father that he has to beat at this game of silence:

> I look down there, and Dad, he's already done eating. He's just sitting there at the end of the table kind of like this. (Everts

---

[9]It is difficult to capture the playful agility of this narrative voice in print. The italicized portions (including those in the Appendix) are the thoughts of the narrator as he is embedded in the story; they are his observations and thoughts as the scene unfolds around him, which contrasts with the voice of the performing raconteur. What is readily apparent in the oral text—Everts's meaningful looks and raised tone, signifying a younger voice—is lacking in an unformatted transcription, so I have attempted to hint at the multiple dimensions of the narrative through italics.

crosses his hands over chest.) Kind of rocking. Looking at me. I'm like, *I'm not doing these fucking dishes, dude.* He's just a-rocking, you know. *I bet I know a way to get him to talk.*

This is the turning point of the story, when the narrator's persona transforms from that of passive inexperience to active performance. The narrator is stirred to action by the pose of the patriarch, and it is at this moment that he is able to sexually perform with an escalating intensity: "I kind of snuggled over a little closer to the girl ... I kind of got a little rougher ... Hell, we just start having our way right there in front of the family! And Dad ain't saying nothing!" With obvious oedipal shades, the young man overthrows the father with a direct challenge to his authority. When the father sees the Vaseline, the implication of sodomy—a violent sexual threat—causes him to admit defeat. He is out-manned by the newcomer in this battle of masculine sexual aggression. In this narrative space, the father is compromised by the young man's burgeoning virility. The symbolic details of the story confirm and amplify the sexual drama of the narrative. The motorcycle, as an emblem of rebellion and challenge, requires a particular kind of maintenance that ultimately helps the young man to overthrow the father's rule. Similarly, the other trappings of the 'bad boy' (like the leather biker's jacket) are what give the narrator power. These icons allude to common stereotypes that are instantly recognizable to Everts's audience and laden with meaning. In the story, it is only by adopting this transgressive persona and through these objects that he is able to have the girl he has been pining for—and her mother to boot. The outward signs confirm his inward transformation.

Significantly, Everts's narrative resists a strict generic definition. Is it a personal narrative or another kind of tale? In her consideration of the nature and form of certain stories, Sandra Dolby Stahl describes the three defining features of personal narratives: "(1) dramatic narrative structure, (2) a consistently implied assertion that the narrative is true, and (3) the self-same identity of the teller and the story's main character" (15). Everts's story satisfies all of these requirements. There is a clear beginning, middle and end with a coherent desire/conflict motivating the narrator (a courtship quest). The veracity of the tale was sworn by Everts as well as his family. In fact, the parents of the story were said to have been at the Ozark River Storytelling event earlier that day. "They're your neighbors, Chip!" one Everts shouted to Forrest Marsden. Finally, the story is told by its main character.

Nate Everts's rhetorical strategy contains certain textual triggers that work to secure the audience's belief in the reality of the story. Everts spends a considerable amount of time setting up the motorcycle purchase.

He buys the motorcycle from the school nurse who is instantly recognized by those natives of the area. He takes the time to explain the fairness of the deal and how the nurse explained the bike's mechanical failings. "She said, just—but I don't know, you know," Everts says, "she was just being honest." He grounds the opening of the story in concrete details and familiar figures, establishing his credibility and specific situation. These mimetic references, along with the true identity of the dirty-dishes family, emphasize the personal elements of the narrative, and Everts makes use of rhetorical triggers in order to secure his audience's belief.

However, when evaluating the other elements of "The Motorcycle," the story bears a considerable resemblance to other traditional narratives. When asked after the event about Everts's narrative, Forrest Marsden remarked that he was sure there was no way it could be true; Nate was just a good storyteller. Forrest shared that afterwards Ben Probert—another participant—had mentioned hearing a similar tale about someone else. The concept of variation comes into play along with the audience's dubious response. In *Folkloristics*, Robert A. Georges and Michael Owen Jones describe traditional bawdy jokes that are structured similarly to Everts's narrative—jokes which play on the male/female dynamics of a group. Georges and Jones write that, in one study done in the mid 1970s, "men's jokes tend to be longer, more narrative in form" than those that had been told by women (215). The writers also note that men tended to enjoy large, public audiences (215). Both of these elements are at work in Everts's performance at the Ozark River Storytelling event. While performed as a personal narrative, the nature of the content, rising humor, and punchy last line of the story lend it the air of a traditional joke. The story's hybridized form features different kinds of narrative structures that make it difficult to definitively classify.

Part personal story, part joke, Nate Everts's narrative also bears a resemblance to earlier folktales in this region. There are compelling similarities between "The Motorcycle" and the old Ozark tales collected by Vance Randolph in the early- and mid-1900s. His bawdy collection of folktales titled *Pissing in the Snow* contains one such tale that, when compared with "The Motorcycle," shows how traditional Ozark themes and sexual politics are still very much alive in the stories told today. "It Didn't Cost Him Nothing" is a folktale Randolph collected in 1953 from Fred High of Berryville, Arkansas. High originally heard the tale near Green Forest, Arkansas around the turn of the century. In this story, two boys see a husband, wife, and daughter walking down the road, and one boy lays down this bet to the other: "I bet you five dollars I can screw that girl, right before her folks, and not cost me a cent" (27). Cunningly, the young man then offers a second bet to the father, saying, "I bet five dollars I can lift all three of you, if you will lay still like I say" (27-28). The boy then stacks the family one on top of the other, with the girl on top, and he has his way with her with the unwitting father unable to see what is going on. While the young man buttons up his pants, he admits defeat and pays the father. Of course, the friend must cover the bet after that: "The way it turned out, the boy from Green Forest just broke even, and he got to screw the pretty girl for nothing" (28).[10]

High's narrative casts the father-figure as the primary opponent that must be overcome and tricked. High's narrative concludes with a message for his listeners: "It just goes to show that a smart young fellow can get pretty near anything he wants in this world, if he knows how to go after it" (28). Just as Everts outmatches the father in "The Motorcycle," the young man in "It Didn't Cost Him Nothing" tricks the old man with a wager and wins the pleasure of the pretty young daughter. This motif can be found in numerous folktales throughout the world, classified as Type 1563, "Both?" in the Aarne-Thompson index. In both Ozark stories, the rebellious, clever young man outwits the father and gets the girl by the end. It is a celebration of youthful ingenuity, determination, and virility. These old values have been passed down, emphasized, and reaffirmed in the tales shared by the Ozark riverside today.

The concept of the wager proves particularly important when comparing High's folktale to Everts's narrative. In "The Motorcycle," the narrator and the girl are going all the way at the dinner table and he thinks to himself, *"Hell we've done the—done our deal."* The boy in High's narrative "broke even" and got the added pleasure of a girl in the process (28). Sex and betting are explicitly linked in these stories, a thematic move that suggests a close connection between challenges and sexual conquest. In both stories, sex is a tool by which young men can get the upper hand in their dealings with older patriarchs. In these narratives courtship—the ultimate test for young men—is equally about virility, clever manipulation, and competition.

Within the context of the larger storytelling festival, "The Motorcycle" generates social meaning as it enters the public imagination. As the festival went on, more and more participants shared stories about relationships and romance. Nate Everts even shared another courtship story, this time about his young daughter, Kylie, and her admirers, who are now being scared off by her older brother, Lane. John Lawson told a story about a

---

[10]In his annotations of Randolph's collection, Frank A. Hoffmann notes that a more widespread version of "It Didn't Cost Him Nothing" leaves out the wager, and some versions describe the youth having intercourse with both daughter and wife (28).

vacation with Melissa, his wife, and Dave Everts, his cousin, when they went down to Arkansas for some Texas music; he describes Dave's ineffective attempts to romance his wife, Tonjia, with a hot bath. Then, the Everts as a group shared the story about an incident in which youths vandalized their campsite across the river, and Nate caught the kids wrecking the old "Love Bus," where the Everts boys used to take their dates back in the day.

These courtship stories reflect the social dynamic of the group as members confirm their social and romantic relationships with one another in the midst of competition. These familiar tropes and plots—the hapless husband, the brash young suitors, long-suffering wives—become points of departure for other stories, relating one person's experience to another's and tightening the bonds of the group through shared stories. In her rhetorical folklore studies, Kathleen Glenister Roberts discusses the importance of paying attention to the "progression from private story to public narrative," noting the complicated power of texts to shape "human decision-making and social life" (131). She writes that narratives are not merely "superorganic entit[ies]" but conceptual systems that influence and reflect social reality (134). Narratives articulate and generate meaning, allowing raconteurs and their audiences to reevaluate or affirm their social relationships. At the Ozark River Storytelling event, courtship narratives offered participants the opportunity to bond over the shared experiences of youthful dalliances, forming connections between groups of people who had not met prior to the event. In *The Politics of Storytelling*, Michael Jackson echoes this idea: "By constructing, relating and sharing stories, people contrive to restore viability to their relationship with others" (18). Storytelling is an invitation to inhabit a social world that is constantly being renegotiated, reframed, and redesigned with every interpersonal exchange. The Ozark River Storytelling courtship stories also allowed the group to work through complicated sexual politics—old lovers, maturing children, rekindled romance—and build a communal sensibility in the present context.

Conclusion

In *Vernacular Voices: The Rhetoric of Publics and Public Spheres*, Gerard A. Hauser writes: "We develop our sense of whether beliefs and values are stable or shifting; what is socially safe or dangerous, expected or prohibited; and what different segments of society believe and espouse through participation in a mosaic of mundane social exchanges and observations" (4). He describes a kind of communal sensibility even as he acknowledges the "shifting" sense of tradition and values. Everyday conversations and stories act as touchstones, allowing us to work through the nebulous, abstract elements of our vernacular culture even as we consider how the material elements of our culture gain symbolic meaning through our social exchange. Stories are generative in this way: they motivate listeners and raconteurs to explore their situations and relationships, forging or reaffirming social networks that are continuously being negotiated from context to context.

My review of the Ozark River Storytelling event highlights the material and imaginative elements that play a role in the cultivation and maintenance of the social relationships among these Ozark participants. The foodways which celebrated local economy, the impromptu festival stations, the bawdy folktales, the courtship narratives: all of these things brought people together to form what is essentially a folk group. Richard Bauman describes the "social matrix" that helps to configure group formation, and he urges folklorists "to conceptualize the social base of folklore in terms of the actual place of the lore in social relationships and its use in communicative interaction" (qtd. in Sims and Stephens 36). By describing and evaluating the folk objects, texts, and customs of the Ozark River Storytelling group, I am working to explicate the social relations that give rise to these artifacts so that I can better understand how folklore still operates amongst living, modern folk groups. Narratives shape these relationships and allow groups to work through unstable social situations, drawing on traditional structures, motifs, or anxieties in order to strengthen the bonds between new people. The study of folklore narratives in public situations reveals how personal stories gain social significance as meaning is generated within a context-specific communal sensibility.

Ozark folklore is alive today. It is at play in the everyday conversations amongst nurserymen like Forrest Marsden and Ben Probert; in the ribald tales of Ozark clans like the Everts; in family heirlooms such as Jeff Wilks's Winchester lever-action rifle that was allegedly given to his grandfather by Jesse James; in the arrowhead fields and mudpuppy-rich waters of Spring River.[11] Popular pastimes have been incorporated into the social matrix of these folk groups,[12] and many traditional elements of Ozark life have been eschewed for more modern conveniences. But the adaptive customs and vibrant stories I have described demonstrate how tradition can be encoded in innovative ways: within social and narrative structures that arise in public festivals. We should encourage Ozark folklore researchers and collectors to explore the living, active, impactful artifacts and stories that

---

[11]See Figure 5 in the Appendix.

[12]For example, corn-holing is something played on many college campuses across the country and not unique to the Ozarks.

are around us today rather than relying predominantly on preservationist methods of study that isolate examples in the distant past. Alongside this, we should consider the ways in which festivals and modern events can reveal how a traditional culture can adapt, evolve, and be negotiated in a public space. Public folklore events (such as the Ozark River Storytelling event) allow us to see context-specific communal sensibilities that are developed and, crucially, also displayed in real-time: a critical perspective which emphasizes the living nature of folklore. Social networks are formed and performed in new contexts at these public events, offering folklorists the opportunity to engage with traditions that are still embedded in the lives of folk groups today. There is a wealth of possibility for this kind of study amidst the old Ozark hills and along the riverside. It is time to celebrate these living traditions.

Appendix

What follows is a transcript of Nate Everts's narrative, "The Motorcycle," and assorted materials from the Ozark River Storytelling alongside photographs of the event taken by Madeline Marsden. Figure numbers correspond with certain portions of the article text.

"The Motorcycle"

Told by Nate Everts of La Russell, Missouri, on March 26, 2016. Offered as a true story, with some good-natured participant skepticism. Everts described it as the "short version" of the tale. The explicit language has not been altered or substituted in order to demonstrate the context-specific sensibility at play in the performance.

I wanted a motorcycle really bad. But I never did really worry about getting one, but a lot worse I wanted to date this girl I wanted to go out with really bad. I wasn't very cool, and she liked cool guys. And I couldn't really impress her very good. So I just kinda give up.

Well then this motorcycle come up, and I had our nurse at the school, her husband had passed away, and he rode this motorcycle all his life. I went up to buy this motorcycle from her, and she's like: "Yeah, you know, Nate—yeah, that'd be good, you know. I'd like to sell you that bike—I think Dale'd be glad you had it," and all this.

I said, "Is there anything wrong with it, you know?"

She said, "Nate, the only thing I know is that it takes in water somewhere. Somewhere on it." She said, "I don't know where it's at; Dale could never find it." She said when it would rain, that bike would not run. She said, "It'd get water on it, somewhere, you know, something, I don't know." She said, "Dale always—all he'd ever do was take some Vaseline, and he kept it with him, and he would just wipe that pan down around the fuel tank. And she said that it shed the water and never had any problems. She said, just—but I don't know, you know, she was just being honest.

I said, "Well alright," you know.

Hell I didn't think nothing of it—hell, I had a motorcycle, you know. I was like *Dumb and Dumber*, you know, riding this sonbitch. I didn't know how to ride.

Well, so anyway, I got the hang of it, you know, and I was driving around—man, this was pretty cool, you know. This other girl I'd really been wanting to go on a date, and I was like, *Man, she might like this.*

So anyway, I go. I go get me a jacket, you know. One of them cool, like, a biker jacket, you know. Like, gonna be cool. And, yeah, leather. And so I got me one of them black coats and I had—yeah, I'd stop down at the grocery store and have me a little Vaseline I kept in my coat.

So this girl, she worked up 'ere at the store, and I'm gonna pull in there. So I pulled in there, you know. I was being cool, you know, had my little helmet on and stuff. Pulled in there, and I got off my motorcycle, you know.

She's like, "Oh my gosh, Nate. Is that your motorcycle?"

And I'm like, "Yeah, you know."

"Well that's cool, you know."

And we visited about it, you know. First time she really ever even talked to me.

"S'alright, you know." So I was like, "Well, you know, would you like to go on a ride some night?"

"Yeah! Yeah."

"Well alright." You know. Man, I was pumped up, you know. So I said, "When? Where?"

She said, "Well just come by my house Friday night. Seven o'clock."

"Okay."

Man I was excited. I'd been looking forward to that all my whole life. I go to pick her up and she comes outside, and she goes, "Nate, we can't."

I said, "Well, you know, are you ready?"

And she's like, "Well, we can't go yet." She said, "My mom and dad want us to eat dinner with them."

"Well that's fine, you know. I'm cool with that. Hell, let's go in and eat, you know."

She's like, "No, no, no." I mean, she wouldn't let me even close to the door. "No, no, no," you know. "You can't go in."

I'm like, "Why?"

She's like, "My ... you know ... our ... my family's different, you know. We're different."

"We all are, you know." I was ready to go on the date. I didn't care. I was ready to go on this date.

And so anyway, she wouldn't let me go in. Finally I'm like, "Listen," I said. "I guarantee you if I go in there there's nothing I've never seen or whatever before." I said, "It'll be fine. We'll go in there; we'll eat supper with them; we'll go watch a movie."

"Okay." She's like, "I'm gonna tell ya." She said there's no talking. She said the first person that talks at the dinner table has to do dishes.

I said, "Alright," you know. "Whatever." In we go.

I walk in the house, and there is fucking dishes everywhere. I mean there's dishes in the closet. There's dishes going up the stairs. Like, we're walking down the hallway and there's dirty dishes everywhere! And I'm like, I mean everywhere you look there's dishes! And I'm like, *There's no way, you know. I'm not saying a word.* But I'm pretty social, you know. I like to talk. I'm like, *Man. I just want to get out of here. I want to go watch movie with her,* you know.

And there was—fucking, we go in the dining room: there's dishes. The kitchen table's full of dirty dishes—everything's got dirty dishes on it. And I'm like ...

And we walk in there, and it's like a normal thing. They're sitting down. Dad's sitting down. Brother's sitting down. They're all sitting around the table. Here comes Mom, bringing the stuff over on the table. And I just kind of walked in. They all kind of, you know. Gave me the nod. Never said a word. *Man this is pretty fucking awkward.*

So we all sit down at the table there, and everybody's passing food around. Every once in a while spoon hits the plate or something, you know. Don't say nothing. And everybody starts eating.

She was right. This was fucked up. Sitting there. And nobody's saying nothing!

Hell, I mean, hour-and-a-half goes by, and it's just like, *Goddamn, I'm ready to get out of here.* Nobody say nothing. I look down there, and Dad, he's already done eating. He's just sitting there at the end of the table kind of like this. (Everts crosses his hands over chest.) Kind of rocking. Looking at me. I'm like, *I'm not doing these fucking dishes, dude.* He's just a-rocking, you know. *I bet I know a way to get him to talk.*

So anyway. I kind of snuggled over a little closer to the girl. She sort of snuggled up there, too. Kind of started rubbing her leg a little bit, you know. Man, she starts kind of getting into it, you know. Well Dad, he's just sitting down there just giving me the old stare. Looking at me. S'pecting him to say something. Man I'm ready to get the hell out of here, but I'm not doing dishes.

I kind of got rougher; I'm going a little more. Man, she just gets worked up—hell, she goes rubbing back! I'm like, *Oh shit,* you know. Hell, we just start having our way right there in front of the family! And Dad ain't saying nothing! I mean this sonbitch ain't talking. I mean, there's fucking—every time the chair would hit, the dishes would rattle! And so anyway, I'm like, *Hell we've done the—done our deal.* And I'm like, *Well shit, I'd still like to go watch a movie,* you know. Dad ain't saying nothing. I thought, *I'll bet I get Dad to talk.*

So I just kind of walked down over at the table. Mom, she was sitting there. She was kind of looking at me funny. I started rubbing on her shoulders. Man, she starts getting into it. I'm like, *Holy shit,* you know. *This ain't really happening to me,* you know.

Well, I'm like rubbing her shoulders and she starts getting into it. The next thing I know—goddang, we're going at it, and I'm like, *Wha*—you know. I'm like in heaven.

Well, all of a sudden, the biggest damn streak of lightning, clap of thunder, hit. *Oh sonofabitch,* you know. I forgot my fucking Vaseline on my bike. So I went over there and got my coat off the chair, put my coat on, grabbed that jar of Vaseline—Dad stood up and said, "I'll do dishes."

Ozark River Storytelling

Please join us on
Saturday, March 26th, 2016
at noon
for food, fishing, and stories
at the Marsden's Spring River access point.

Story Collector: Mariah Marsden
Hosts: Chip and Cat Marsden
Feel free to email with questions: memzr3@mail.umkc.edu

We're interested in the stories you love to tell:
work stories
family stories
local history
legends
weather stories
jokes
folklore/superstitions
and more.

There are no wrong subjects. Come and share
your favorites with friends and neighbors. The
event is open to anyone interested in sharing
tales or listening to Ozarkers shoot the breeze.

*A few tables, chairs, and snacks/beer will
be provided, but you're welcome to bring
any river gear you'd like to have on hand
(poles, chairs, extra food, etc.).*

We'll have an audio recorder at the site, and we'll provide copies to interested participants. We're also collecting any written/typed stories you might have—something you've scribbled down or kept over the years. Is there a particular story you think of beforehand and you write/type it out? We'd love to collect it!

Mariah is a graduate student at UMKC working on a folklore collection project and gathering stories from her home land. She studies Ozark narratives, folktales, lore, storytelling, and the influence of texts on the local life of La Russell. She also writes fiction inspired by life in southwest Missouri.

FIGURE 1. *Event Invitation produced by Mariah Marsden and distributed by Forrest Marsden*

FIGURE 2. *Larry Chrisman shows off his polished rock collection from the tailgate of his pickup truck. Some of these Missouri flint pieces are arrowheads that have tumbled and polished smooth. Photo by Madeline Marsden.*

FIGURE 3. *This sign greeted guests as they drove down the road to the Marsden access point. Designed and staked by Forrest Marsden, the sly message suggests that "political speaches [sic]" would not be welcome at the event. Behind the sign: the northernmost arrowhead field, which Forrest had tilled for the guests. Photo by author.*

FIGURE 4. *The fire pit with Catherine Marsden's baked beans simmering in a cast-iron pot that had been passed down from her parents. Forrest Marsden fashioned the pit from the rear steel wheel off of an old tractor. Photo by Madeline Marsden.*

FIGURE 5. *The strangest catch of the day: an Ozarks "mudpuppy" caught by David "Dave" Everts. Everyone at the event gathered to see this aquatic salamander and debate about what it was actually called. Catherine Marsden supplied the agreed-upon name. Photos by Madeline Marsden.*

FIGURE 6. *Robert "Bob" Alexander, a member of the Americana band called Joshin the Giants based in southwest Missouri, entertains participants with songs, both classics and original pieces. Photo by Madeline Marsden.*

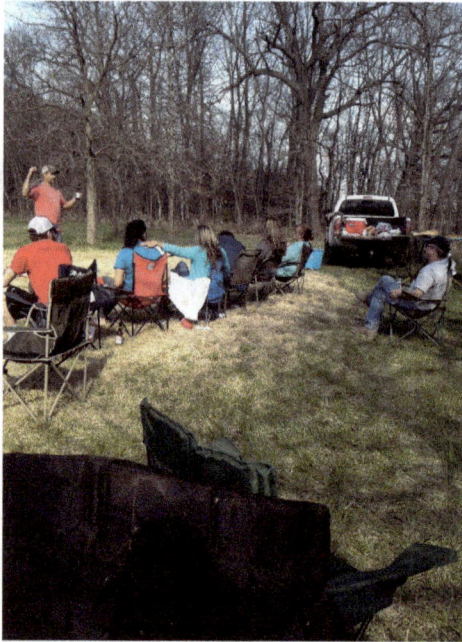

FIGURE 7. *The Everts family sitting in a row, listening to Nate Everts (standing center-stage) tell stories. Nate's fry station is now packed away in the truck (right). Photo by Madeline Marsden.*

FIGURE 8. *The corn-holing field. Forrest Marsden getting ready to toss the bean bag against opponent, Rick Jones (right). The audience watches the show. Photo by Madeline Marsden.*

FIGURE 9. *Rick Jones' toss. Behind him is his patriotic van, which he uses during his gold-panning trips. Photo by Madeline Marsden.*

Bibliography

Abrahams, Roger D. *Everyday Life: A Poetics of Vernacular Practices*. Philadelphia: U of Pennsylvania P, 2005.

Chrisman, Charles and Neva. *The History of LaRussell*. Verona, MO: Johnson Valley Printers, 1988.

Georges, Robert A. and Michael Owen Jones. *Folkloristics: An Introduction*. Bloomington: Indiana UP, 1995.

Hauser, Gerard A. *Vernacular Voices: The Rhetoric of Publics and Public Spheres*. Columbia: U of South Carolina P, 1999.

Herman, David. "Exploring the Nexus of Narrative and Mind." *Narrative Theory: Core Concepts and Critical Debates*. Columbus: Ohio State UP, 2012. 14-19.

Jackson, Michael. *The Politics of Storytelling: Violence, Transgression and Intersubjectivity*. Portland: Museum Tusculanum Press, 2002.

The LaRussell Commercial Club. *A Synopsis of LaRussell, MO*. n.d. Lithographed booklet. Verona, MO: Johnson's Valley Printers, 1988.

Randolph, Vance. *Pissing in the Snow and Other Ozark Folktales*. 1976. Chicago: U of Illinois P, 1986.

Roberts, Kathleen Glenister. "Texturing the Narrative Paradigm: Folklore and Communication." *Communication Quarterly* 52.2 (2004): 129-42. Web. 19 Feb. 2016.

Rossiter, Phyllis. *A Living History of the Ozarks*. Gretna, LA: Pelican, 1992.

Sims, Martha C. and Martine Stephens. *Living Folklore*. 2nd ed. Logan: Utah State UP, 2011.

Stahl, Sandra Dolby. *Literary Folkloristics and the Personal Narrative*. Bloomington: Indiana UP, 1989.

Foodways and Resistance in a Missouri Residential Mental Health Facility (Claire Schmidt and Laurel Schmidt)

Introduction

In his 2005 American Folklore Society presidential address, folklorist Michael Owen Jones pronounced, "Nutrition educators and counselors would benefit from drawing upon ethnographic investigations of the meanings of food in their efforts to design dietary programs, while folklorists should consider adding practical applications of foodways research to their plate" (130). The following preliminary study responds to this challenge, and argues that mental health practitioners in particular can benefit from working with folklorists in order to more *effectively help their clients achieve their health goals.*

Drawing on L. Schmidt's work as a psychiatric social worker at a 16-bed Mid-Missouri transitional Intensive Residential Treatment Setting (IRTS) and C. Schmidt's focus on occupational culture, folklore of institutions, and foodways, this article explores the role of food and foodways for staff and clients in institutions such as IRTS and other residential facilities. We argue that food is an important part of the occupational expressive culture of social workers and at the same time, is a constant source of conflict between staff and the clients they serve. Because food is at the crossroads of public and private, culture, safety, health, and bodily control, it is a source of ongoing conflict among clients and between clients and staff. Food is of-ten perceived as a way of showing caring, and a way of promoting socially appropriate and healthy behavior, but it also triggers conflict (Mishna et al 32). Residential facilities bring together individuals from many different cultures and backgrounds, and cultural attitudes toward food contribute to issues of control and resistance. An incomplete understanding of the role of food in the lives of both clients and care-workers prevents both groups from reframing their often unhealthy relationship with food. Folklorists can help social workers, psychologists, and other public health profession-als understand the social and community power of food. In particular, public folklorists have the opportunity to make foodways a much more visible part of their programming and in doing so they can contribute to a more nuanced understanding of food as a meaningful part of "artistic communication in small groups" (Ben-Amos 14).

As sisters, we share a food culture grounded in our white, rural, Wis-consin upbringing and informed by an ongoing mutual fascination with growing, cooking, eating, and preserving food. We subscribe to cook-ing magazines like *Bon Appetit* and *Cooks Illustrated*; we follow food blogs like "Behind Closed Ovens,"[1] "Serious Eats," and "Smitten Kitchen." As children we gardened and went regularly with our grandmother to the na-tion's largest farmer's market in Madison, Wisconsin. We grew up foraging berries, canning, pickling, and baking bread with our mother. As women in our thirties, we both mock and embrace "hipster food" (see Spiegel's "The 22 Most Hipster Foods on the Planet"). In our family, food can be given as Christmas or birthday gifts. We cook complicated and expensive dishes in honor of our loved ones' birthdays. We always bring a dish to pass. We eat cheese and brats, and we drink beer and old fashioneds at Friday night fish fries in our home state. Having transplanted ourselves to Missouri as adults, we make peach jam and have opinions about the best places to get gooey butter cake and burnt ends. And, as professionals, we share interests and respect each others' calling. One of us is a folklorist with a strong professional interest in social work, the other a social worker with a strong professional interest in folklore.

Literature Review

Folklorists have long understood that food and its preparation, pur-chase, production, and consumption is an important part of expressive

---

[1]Now defunct, though the author, C.A. Pinkham, continues to blog at https://www.thrillist.com/off-the-menu

culture (see Lucy M. Long's introduction to the Winter 2009 issue of the *Journal of American Folklore* for an overview of recent folkloristic scholarship on foodways). Michael Owen Jones has argued that folklorists have a responsibility to bring their understanding of food and identity to the public health arena. As Long points out, folklorists understand food as inherently political; food exists within international contexts of economic and cultural power but also within small-group politics of placement, serving order, and menu choice, as well as cultural politics of food meaning and representation (6). Holly Everett's 2009 article "Vernacular Health Moralities and Culinary Tourism in Newfoundland and Labrador" draws particular attention to the class-based moral and health judgments made by outsiders regarding traditional working-class foodways.

A folkloristic understanding of food and identity can usefully develop a more nuanced understanding of identity within institutions. Erving Goffman's foundational text, *Asylums: Essays on the Social Situation of Mental Patients and Other Inmates* (1961) argues that the pervasive control of total institutions continually bombards the individual with threats to their identity. In response to ongoing identity threat, the patient or inmate adapts to and resists the institution by creating space where he or she can assert autonomy and control. As Ugelvik and others note, food in institutions can be understood as an identity threat (Cross 2009) but food can also be used to create space for resistance of the institution itself and can be an integral part of identity work (Ugelvik 48; Earle and Phillips 2012).

Food is a source of comfort and conflict among incarcerated people in jail and in prison, as social work scholar Amy Smoyer and folklorist Michael Owen Jones have argued. In her 2014 article "Good and Healthy: Foodways and Construction of Identity in a Women's Prison" Smoyer argues that incarcerated women use narratives of food to construct non-criminal identities, at times through their resistance of the food on offer at the institution. In her 2004 article "Dining In: The Symbolic Power of Food in Prison" Rebecca Godderis argues that food and food narratives allow inmates to create consumptive spaces that negotiate and contest power-based inequalities in prison. Their arguments can be usefully applied to other controlled communities like the IRTS where L. Schmidt works.

The relationship between food and mental illness is complex. As Brewerton and others point out, food is a common, legal, method of self-medication for traumatized individuals. Many people with severe mental illness have a history of trauma and use food for comfort and coping. Severe trauma, including sexual abuse and violence, is associated with obesity. Childhood sexual abuse in particular is associated with use of food as a coping mechanism (Taylor et al 9; Harrington et al., 214). People with serious and persistent mental illness are at high risk for obesity. Part of that risk comes from side effects of medication, but many other psychological, physical, and sociological factors influence this risk (see Taylor, et al., 2012 for a review of the recent literature surrounding mental illness and obesity). Mental illness and food insecurity, defined by the United Nations as "the limited or uncertain availability of nutritionally adequate, safe foods or the inability to acquire personally acceptable foods in socially acceptable ways" often co-occur (see Muldoon et al., 2013; Doudna, Reina, and Greder 2015). A history of food insecurity can result in disordered eating patterns, obesity, and food hoarding (see Peterman et al., 2010; Emerson et al., 2009). At the same time, the limited amount of research on social worker attitudes toward obese people suggests that the stigma of obesity can affect social work practice (Lawrence 64).

While an individual's relationship with food is influenced by myriad factors of culture, class, history, and health, in 21st century United States, food and eating is tied to beliefs about and discourses of morality, willpower, and individual self-control (Inthorne and Boyce 90-91; Gard and Wright 7) and these discourses are tied back to larger social contexts encompassing race and class. Eating in a healthy way is being "good" while eating in an unhealthy way is being "bad." Delaney and McCarthy summarize,

> Healthiness represents virtuous living as a moral accomplishment in secular societies while public health and health promotion "may be viewed as contributing to the moral regulation of society, focusing as they do upon ethical and moral practices of the self" (Lupton, 1995, p. 4). Healthism has subsumed some of the religious attitudes towards food resulting in a continued moralising of food behaviours and reinforcement of Christian beliefs around gluttony (Coveney, 2006; Gracia-Arnaiz, 2010; Lupton, 1996). (105)

This discourse of eating in a "good" way is tied directly to issues of race, class, and wealth. As Counihan notes, "class, race, ethnic, and gender boundaries are maintained by eating differences... . Voluntary restraint and freedom of choice toward food differentiate well-fed, well-off people from poor people with hunger and limited ways to satisfy it" (Counihan 126). Thus, obesity (bad) is often associated with poverty, ignorance, and generalized "badness." The current discourses surrounding food, health, and morality threaten to further marginalize an already disenfranchised population: people with severe mental illnesses who reside in IRTS like the ones we focus on in this study or similar residential facilities.

Methodology

Research within the IRTS was conducted by L. Schmidt through a combination of personal observation garnered over one year as a Residential Support Assistant (RSA) and three years as a Community Support Specialist (CSS) and part of the facility's Treatment Team. These observations include both personal interactions with clients relating to food and conversations with clients and staff regarding food. Interviews were conducted with five IRTS staff, whose names have been changed for reasons of confidentiality. These staff include the facility Director, Dana; the Residential Support Assistant (RSA) Supervisor, Carrie; two RNs, Lenora and Samantha; and an RSA, Patricia, who conducts grocery shopping, assists with meal preparation, and for a period of time assisted with menu planning. These staff have been employed at the IRTS for periods of time ranging from six months for one of the RNs to close to five years for the Director; all other staff interviewed have been employed at the facility for at least eighteen months. Interviews were conducted in a group setting and one-on-one.

Our Findings

In the following section we focus first on the ways food functions within this particular IRTS, then we focus on the way clients' relationship with food and eating creates conflict, and finally on the way staff experiences food-related conflicts.

Background

Intensive Residential Treatment Settings are a type of residential facility licensed by Missouri's Department of Mental Health (DMH). IRTS were originally established to function as a step-down program for individuals with serious and persistent mental illness who have been released from long-term intensive treatment at state-run psychiatric hospitals, but who are not yet ready to live independently in their own homes or with family. IRTS are typically designed to be transitional facilities at which clients reside for a period of time—12-24 months at the IRTS in this study—as they prepare for life in the community.

The majority of clients who reside at this facility live under multiple levels of supervision; not only must clients follow facility rules, but many also have court-appointed legal guardians who must be informed of and approve of any significant changes in a client's status, such as medication changes, employment, engagement in a sexual relationship, etc., and have ultimate control over the type of treatment a client receives and where that client may live.

In addition, many clients are involved in the forensic system; they have committed a crime but have been deemed "not guilty by reason of mental disease or defect" for this crime by the courts. These clients are appointed a Forensic Case Monitor (FCM) who exercises a similar level of control over the client that a guardian would have. FCMs monitor their clients closely to ensure that the clients are not in danger of relapse or of becoming a danger to the community at large. Typically, participation in the DMH's forensic system is for life, something that many forensic clients struggle to come to terms with.

Not only must many clients live under the close scrutiny of guardians and/or FCMs, some clients come from even more restrictive and controlled residential environments than this IRTS, and this history also informs their current relationships with food. Forensic clients and others who have been committed to state psychiatric hospitals often experience lengthy periods of institutionalization, ranging from one year to many decades, where clients have very limited control over their food choices. Food is chosen and prepared by hospital staff, though clients may be employed in the kitchens. While in these institutions, some clients are required to follow diabetic diets, low-sodium diets, or other specific dietary guidelines. Other clients have lived for extended periods of time in Residential Care Facilities (RCFs). Many RCFs, unlike settings such as this IRTS, have closed kitchens where the menu is set and non-negotiable and prepared by staff, with designated meal and snack times, with all food choices regulated by the facility. As in hospital settings, clients have limited access to or control over cooking, independent food preparation, meal times, or snack choices; while clients at RCFs are free to purchase snack foods at stores in the community, clients in these facilities tend to have extremely limited spending power as they receive a personal spending allowance ranging from only $30 to no more than $80 per month depending on the facility.

However, at a facility such as this IRTS, food choice, frequency of consumption, and amount is an opportunity for clients to exercise some control when larger choices, such as where and in what setting one lives, whether one can be employed and in what type of work, whether one may drive, whether one may engage in the sexual relationship of one's choice, what medications one must take, which doctors one must see, and what types of treatment one must participate in are made by others.

IRTS are unique residential settings in that, unlike RCFs, clients operate with significant levels of autonomy and independence within the restrictions placed upon them by their guardians and/or FCMs and the facility. RCFs, unlike IRTS, are designed to be long-term care facilities and clients may live their entire adult lives in an RCF. Because there is no expectation of independent, community living for many RCF residents, independent living skills are not emphasized or taught. Many RCFs have staff that prepare all meals and snacks and handle all cooking and cleaning, including washing clients' laundry, in a similar fashion to many nursing homes.

Clients are placed at an IRTS because they are believed to be capable of living independently in the community at a future point. Clients must demonstrate that they are psychiatrically stable, not a risk to the safety and well-being of themselves or the greater community, and that they have learned the independent living skills (such as managing their own medications, scheduling and attending their own doctor's appointments, navigating the Social Security and Medicaid systems in order to maintain benefits, and demonstrating the ability to manage a household, including budgeting, cooking and cleaning) necessary to be successful without staff support. During their time at the IRTS, clients work with staff to develop these skills and abilities.

However, in facilities such as this IRTS, because clients have more independence and more participation in cooking, food selection, and food purchase, food exists in an arena of heightened conflict. The very possibility of a choice, any choice, in a setting where so many choices are made by others and so few factors are within residents' control, renders all choices disproportionately - to an outside observer—valuable and consequently worth fighting over. Staff purchase groceries based on a client-developed grocery list but within limitations placed by accreditation agencies and taking into consideration recommendations from primary care doctors. In order to be accredited by agencies such as the Commission on Accreditation of Rehabilitation Facilities (CARF), a residential facility must adhere to certain nutritional guidelines, such as not serving the same protein two nights in a row and not purchasing "junk" food for clients. Staff at residential facilities such as this IRTS must negotiate a fine line between meeting the requirements of accrediting bodies while still allowing residents independence and ownership of their meals and food preparation necessary to be successful once living independently.

Many residents move to this IRTS from facilities such as state hospitals or RCFS, with little to no control over food consumption. Others move to this facility because they had been living independently but were not successful in doing so, typically because of untreated or unmanaged psychiatric conditions and/or substance abuse, and were referred to this facility by psychiatrists, therapists, or caseworkers. Often these individuals come from backgrounds of food insecurity. Once admitted to this IRTS, many clients demonstrate limited self-control in regard to food consumption; often clients eat to excess by not controlling portion sizes, eat snacks that are the caloric equivalent to meals, or eat multiple servings of dessert on those occasions when dessert is available. Some individuals are able to curb this behavior, perhaps because they lack some of the determining risk factors for obesity, such as a history of trauma, or because they have more developed social and leisure activities, as we discuss later, while others struggle throughout their stay at the facility.

Food & Institutional Expressive Culture

Food is an important part of the expressive culture of the staff at this IRTS and an important part of the expressive occupational culture of social workers and other mental health workers. As in many office settings, food is present at meetings, trainings, going-away parties, birthday celebrations, and "just because"—often in response to particularly emotional or stressful periods at work, such as following a client crisis. Sometimes staff bring food they have prepared at home; other times staff (or the agency itself) will purchase food from area restaurants and grocery stores. Staff share excess produce from their gardens in the summer, bring in leftover Halloween candy on November 1, and exchange cookies at Christmas time. Food is a way that some (though not all) staff express creativity, skill, insight, affection, and insider/outsider status. Food can be a gift, a joke, or an incentive, depending on the context and the audience.

This expressive culture is a product of the institution itself but is influenced by the staff's cultural backgrounds. Many staff come from families where food is very important socially and culturally. The Director, Dana, explained that in her family culture, food serves as a means of "showing love or affection" and that family members would want to buy treats for their young relatives that they themselves either weren't permitted or could not afford when they were that age. RSA Supervisor, Carrie, agreed with this, but went on to explain that on one side of her family food is socially and culturally important and that family gatherings always involve food and meals, but that on the other side of her family food is not culturally important. When L. Schmidt asked what replaced food as the cultural foundation, Carrie stated, succinctly "fighting."

Some staff bring their family-food culture to work with them. Certain staff will cook desserts or special treats for clients, possibly in an attempt to demonstrate affection and caring for those clients or in hopes of generating good-will, despite the fact that these foods are not healthy options for clients and that many clients will overindulge on these foods which may pose a legitimate health risk for diabetic clients. As an RSA, L. Schmidt assisted clients in cooking muffins, cakes, and other similar items for those clients to take with them to church meals, an extension both of L. Schmidt's family-food culture and the client's food culture.

The food-based expressive culture of the IRTS is marked by high fat and sugar. Desserts are by far the most common food brought to share among staff and clients. Cookies, bars, cake, and candy are considered "normal" food to bring to eat at a party, meeting, or other gathering at the facility. Pizza, barbeque, and fast-food are typical foods provided at staff meetings or trainings. While staff may gather (without their clients) at a restaurant or bar, food ordered to share in this situation will be likely high in fat (such as onion rings or jalapeno poppers) but lower in sugar. These foods are very much in evidence during periods of high stress. L. Schmidt baked and brought in a variety of cookies after a particularly emotionally and men-tally fatiguing week, while Carrie and Dana have brought in doughnuts for staff for similar reasons. This demonstrates that while staff have attempted to break the "food as a reward" culture among clients, as will be discussed later, this culture is yet strongly evident between and among staff; the mentality of having "earned" a high-calorie treat as a result of having sur-vived a difficult and trying experience, may be a significant contributing factor to the previously discussed high rates of obesity among care work-ers, as high-stress, high-risk, emotionally-wearing episodes are the norm rather than the exception in these professions.

While these food choices mirror those of typical United States office cultures, the choices of fast food or snack food are often made out of a ne-cessity for sustenance that can be obtained and eaten quickly, as staff may have no more than five minutes to eat between appointments and may be required to eat in the car while transporting clients. Because each client tends to have myriad psychiatric, therapeutic, and physical care providers, clients have multiple appointments per month and very few clients are able to attend appointments on their own. As appointments must be scheduled around the availability of the provider, often IRTS staff are faced with the choice of several back-to-back appointments or a delay of months before a client can see that provider. In addition to scheduling issues, clients re-quire assistance on an unplanned basis, such as becoming ill, having family emergencies, or experiencing crises that require inpatient hospitalization, a process that takes many hours. Lunches are often eaten while one works at a desk writing case notes. Because of the unpredictable nature of men-tal health work, staff rely more heavily on fast food or hastily-eaten snack foods than do people in conventional office settings.

Notably, when staff do find themselves with time to sit down and eat lunch, they do so together, often all ordering food from one restaurant, sitting at one table and using this time to discuss family, friends, and personal stressors, strengthening the interpersonal relationships between staff, much as families may do at the evening meal. Because staff, especially the clinical Treatment Team members, must work closely together under situations of extreme stress and emotion and must, at all times, present a united front to clients, these opportunities to bond over the shared culture of food may serve to make the team more effective in the professional arena.

Clients also participate in the expressive food culture of the institution. Clients will cook for each other outside of designated meal preparation, in order to gain acceptance or value within the culture of the residential facility (see Earle and Phillips [2012] for similar findings in a medium-security English men's prison); these foods are almost exclusively desserts or sweets, though fried chicken is a notable exception. Staff have also observed that interaction among and between clients is very different on those holidays where all clients and staff work together to prepare a "family-style" meal, where all or most clients contribute to the preparation and serving of a communal meal. Patricia, an RSA closely involved in grocery shopping, meal planning, and preparation, explained that there are "no arguments, [clients] sit down, eat as a family. It's a different mindset – working as a team, being involved," and postulated that this may remind clients of "memories of family meals" in the past, possibly before the onset of serious mental illness and/or substance abuse. Meals, especially holiday meals where all clients have ownership of and participate in the preparation of the meal, may serve to emulate the meals that clients enjoyed as part of their family or social unit and these "family-style" meals with peers may serve as a cultural substitute for the family unit.

Client Resistance

For clients, food is a site of resistance. Smoyer (2016) has demonstrated that incarcerated women use food to resist institutional control, and Smoyer's findings support L. Schmidt's observations in her workplace. Both staff and clients in residential settings cite the importance to clients of being able to control all aspects of their food consumption. This client goal is often in conflict with staff goals of creating an environment of healthy food options and choices as part of an overall approach toward wellness. In order to help clients maintain overall wellness and stability, staff, Forensic Case Monitors (FCMs), guardians, and parole officers control clients' access to drugs, alcohol, and sex. Food choice and amount remains largely under the control of the client, though often clients are provided with dietary recommendations by primary care doctors or dieticians and some restrictions are placed on what food items are purchased by the facility, though no restrictions are placed on food that clients purchase for themselves.

The food culture among clients at this IRTS has two distinct components: the desired food culture imposed by staff and in part dictated by licensing and accrediting bodies, and the food culture among and between clients. The former includes the previously discussed limitations on what groceries will be purchased by the facility, as well as attempts by staff to change the existing food culture of clients through education. The facility-imposed food culture is constantly evolving as the IRTS staff attempt to meet changing requirements of accrediting and similar agencies. An example of this evolution is the change in client rewards or incentives. At this IRTS, when a client performs a kind or helpful act above and beyond their typical assigned tasks, such as doing another resident's chore if that individual is ill or helping another resident make dinner, other clients or staff may give that client a "kudos." When L. Schmidt began at this IRTS as an RSA in 2012, the kudos took the form of a Hershey's chocolate bar. As staff realized that this reinforcement of the "food as reward" mentality may exacerbate an already unhealthy relationship with food that exists among some clients, as well as not conforming to the expectations of accrediting or licensing bodies, the kudos reward system was altered so that a client who had been given a kudos received a praiseful post-card instead. As clients felt this reward to be profoundly unsatisfactory, clients now receive an entry in a drawing for a gift card for each kudos they receive, a compromise that both clients and staff appear to find acceptable. It is noteworthy that while staff have attempted to break the cycle of rewarding client effort through treats, staff, as previously discussed, continue to reward themselves and each other through food. This can create an additional source of conflict between staff and clients, as clients observe staff bringing pizza, doughnuts, cookies, cupcakes, and other coveted treats for themselves from which clients are restricted. While staff, when clients inevitably comment upon these items, remind clients that they are free to purchase or make their own "treats," this does not fully diminish the perceived power differential; indeed, it serves to underline the disparity in buying power between clients, who, unless employed, receive a $60/month spending allowance—and staff.

Staff encourage clients to make healthy food choices and provide education on what constitutes healthy choices. This education is primarily provided by RNs and by L. Schmidt, as the Community Support Specialist, though RSA staff provide the day-to-day support, encouragement, and reinforcement that many clients require as these are the staff present at mealtimes and during the evening and night when snacking is most prevalent. L. Schmidt has provided assistance to clients using both professional and personal perspectives; professionally, she has provided clients with print-outs of the U.S. Department of Agriculture's MyPlate tool[2] and reviewed and explained these dietary guidelines to clients, as well as teaching clients how to read nutritional labels and what each category of macro and micronutrient is, educating clients on weight loss myths, such as the inefficacy of the "Master Cleanse," providing visual references of portion sizes to clients, and explaining the 2,000 calorie per day suggested caloric intake and how this may vary from individual to individual. On a personal level, L. Schmidt has shared her own struggles with healthy eating, lifestyle changes that have helped her to maintain a healthy weight, such as calorie tracking, the physical and mental health benefits of a consistent fitness routine, and humorous stories of times that she was successful or unsuccessful in maintaining her healthy eating and exercise habits, such as "accidentally" eating an entire box of Oreos. However, clients often resist these recommendations or intentionally misinterpret them. As Dana, Carrie, Lenora, and Samantha agreed, some individuals "just don't care." Dana expanded on this, explaining that for some clients this is due to the Stage of Change[3] at which they are regarding healthy food choices; "it's just not important or a value to some people" at this point in their lives. Carrie agreed, stating that clients "want what they want in the moment, and don't care about consequences." Other clients will willfully misinterpret their doctor's recommendations; as Dana related, people "hear what they want to hear—'oh, I need my diabetic snack.'" Samantha interjected that clients will then "eat a whole meal" rather than a snack. This was echoed by Patricia's sardonic statement that clients "just don't give a damn," especially about "long-term consequences." Patricia went on to cite some clients' refusal to be educated despite the opportunities provided to them, feeling that this is a form of "resistance." Patricia also explained that, "we give them meds to fix things: you're depressed? Here's a pill for that." Referencing one young female client who has gained over 80lb since her

---

[2]http://www.choosemyplate.gov/

[3]A model used to identify how prepared an individual is to make a change in behavior and to determine the stage at which an individual is in the process of change, which informs how staff intervene with the individual. Originally developed as a smoking cessation model: Prochaska, J. and DiClemente, C. (1983) Stages and processes of self-change in smoking: toward an integrative model of change. *Journal of Consulting and Clinical Psychology*, 5, 390–395.

arrival at the IRTS, Patricia said that she "just wants a pill" for her weight loss and would expect a weight loss pill to "work as quickly" as an anti-anxiety medication.

However, all staff interviewed were universal in agreement that control is the primary factor in all food-related conflict at the IRTS. As Carrie pointed out, and to which RNs Lenora and Samantha agreed, resisting recommendations gives clients an opportunity to show that staff "can't tell me what to do." As Roberts and Bailey note, locus of control is a key factor in both barriers and incentives for healthy lifestyle choices among people with severe mental illness (Roberts and Bailey 702-703). Resistance is an understandable and expected response, and competing version of "normal" are common (see Coffey 2011).

Food-related conflicts may also stem from a sense of earned entitlement. While some clients of this IRTS and other residential facilities reside in these settings voluntarily, the majority are required by their guardians or Forensic Case Monitors to live in supervised settings. Residing in such a facility is not inexpensive, especially in facilities such as IRTS where 24/7 awake staff, RN services and community support services are provided, as well as amenities such as wi-fi and cable TV. The cost of room, board, and care exceeds $1,000 per month at this IRTS. Typically, the Department of Mental Health requires that this is paid for by the resident's Social Security benefits with additional funding provided by DMH to make up any difference. Clients who are forced to live in a facility feel an added sense of unfairness when they are required to spend all of their benefits to do so. This contributes to a sense of entitlement regarding what food is purchased. As Carrie put it, many clients think, and some verbalize, "I give you all my money, you should buy what I tell you to." Clients take umbrage to restrictions on what staff can buy when grocery shopping—limitations include no purchasing of soda, candy, coffee, etc, and very limited purchasing of prepackaged items, such as frozen pizzas, chicken nuggets, etc—telling staff that as their money pays for the groceries, they should be able to choose what is purchased.

Clients may also feel a sense of earned entitlement unrelated to their finances; as Patricia suggested, for individuals who have been institutionalized, "being able to control the amount [of food] and what it is is like a reward. They get to pick what they want and have options—it's an excitement." Clients who have progressed through the state hospital system, especially those clients who were initially committed to maximum security institutions and worked their way through medium and minimum security to ultimately be admitted to an open-campus IRTS, may feel that they have earned the right to choose what, when, and how they eat.

In addition, many clients in this and other residential facilities have historical experiences that impact their relationships with food, including extended periods of homelessness and/or food insecurity and histories of sexual or physical abuse. These individual histories contribute to a need on the part of clients to maintain control both over what enters their bodies and over their physical appearance, including perceived physical attractiveness. Individuals with a history of sexual abuse have been noted to attempt to make themselves unattractive as victims, to reduce the likelihood of future abuse (see Brewerton 2011). When discussing clients' unhealthy relationships with food, Dana stated that "it's like on that show, "My 600-pound Life," the things those people are trying to deal with" when discussing the impacts of physical and emotional trauma on client relationships with food.

Control, as it relates to food choices, can be demonstrated in a variety of ways within a residential facility. Some of these conflicts are overt, such as arguments between staff and clients over why the facility does not purchase certain food items and verbal or physical conflicts between clients over highly-prized food items or disagreements about food preparation; or covert, such as food hiding or hoarding.

Food and Client Conflict

Clients can at times use food as a means of demonstrating control over each other. Staff have observed clients intentionally eating all of one specific type of food, in part to ensure that other clients cannot have access to this type of food. Patricia described one client who ate an entire box of maple-brown-sugar instant oatmeal in one sitting, explaining that she felt he had done this in part to be "malicious" and that he did so "on purpose" so that no other clients could enjoy this item and that this type of behavior "sometimes causes [verbal] fights between clients, because someone ate all of something they hadn't had any of."

When L. Schmidt interviewed the treatment team, including Carrie and Lenora, several staff recalled when an RSA found a tub of butter substitute with a spoon in it in a cupboard, hidden behind other items where fellow clients would be less likely to find and consume this item. Later interviews revealed that this was a repeated, rather than one-time, behavior on the part of an unknown client. These incidents are most frequent when the food in question is a "prized" food, such as snack food or dessert. Patricia noted that certain types of food, such as veggie straws, may be "more likely to cause problems with people who have been institutionalized," perhaps because these foods "have more value" and that clients get "more defensive" about these foods. Clients may seek to obtain the maximum amount of that item possible for themselves. At this IRTS one client physically assaulted another, fracturing the client' ribs, following a verbal altercation over whether or not the second client was planning to keep to herself a bag of nuts that had been purchased while grocery shopping for the facility.

As one of the purposes of an IRTS is to teach life skills, such as cooking, clients at this IRTS are required to cook dinner on a rotation for the entire facility. Cooking for other residents is a constant area of conflict. On nights when a client cooks it is typical for that client to use this opportunity to demonstrate control over their peers by serving themselves before allowing others to begin dishing up, or by dictating portions to their peers. Food thereby serves as a means of retaining control over oneself and having control over others, even if for a limited duration. At times there is a risk that the evening meal will become contentious when clients object to other clients having this temporary power over what they will eat. At this IRTS, one client became so incensed at another client's method of preparing fried rice that she called 911 multiple times. While this is an extreme example, it is rare for a week to go by without clients complaining about the evening meal.

Because clients come from varying cultural backgrounds and have varying comfort levels in terms of cooking, the evening meal will vary from frozen, heated chicken or fish patties served with frozen vegetables and canned fruit, simple grilled meats with canned baked beans, to made-from-scratch fish tacos, fried chicken, or pizza. Many clients with limited cooking experience and whose meals up until their admission at this facility have consisted of reheated frozen entrees, struggle to come to terms with new, more adventurous dishes, and may refuse to try these meals, often calling them "weird." As the meals that are refused are typically those made from scratch and that are culturally important to the cook, this refusal serves as an additional source of conflict and can lead to verbal disputes and hurt feelings. Indeed, as Samantha related to L. Schmidt recently after a client had cooked fish tacos that most residents refused to try, "I didn't want to eat, but I couldn't let [the cook] sit there and eat by herself when no one else was. And they were yummy." This incident illustrates both how "weird" food, that is to say food outside of one's own cultural norms, can be a source of client-client conflict but also an opportunity for staff to demonstrate an acceptance of a client's personal or family culture.

Staff-Client Food Conflict

Conflicts between staff and client are rarely dramatic. Instead, conflict over food is an ever-present, low-level source of tension. Clients often feel resentment toward staff because of limitations placed on foods purchased, especially snack foods, and limitations on menu planning, such as restrictions on how often deep-fried foods or desserts can be prepared. One client complained to L. Schmidt, Dana, and Carrie because he could not prepare pizza the night after a peer had made biscuits and gravy, because both meals used sausage. This is very typical of the type of interaction between staff and clients regarding the menu. Dana reminded the client that this is a rule that the facility cannot control as it is set by CARF, the accrediting body. Generally clients can be redirected by reminders like this, especially as they serve to minimize the power differential between clients and staff, whereas a reaction from staff such as "because we said so" would only serve to stir up conflict.

The opposite complaint can also be heard; once pork was served multiple days in a week and one client complained to Carrie about the frequency of this preparation, knowing that this was against facility regulations. Carrie acknowledged that this was a mistake on the part of staff and that though staff try to be careful in the menu, "we're all human, everyone makes mistakes." The client acknowledged this and the matter was dropped.

However, these examples serve to illustrate that though a food issue may appear negligible, for clients food is a serious source of frustration and can lead to serious resistance. Because control over food is so highly prized by clients, even infringements on this control that may appear minor to outsiders are taken very seriously.

Portion control often leads to staff-client conflict. It is not atypical for two or three clients to eat the entirety of an item meant to serve sixteen people. This then becomes a source of client conflict as those clients who did not have opportunity to eat these foods become upset. Clients have, however, reported finding attempted enforcement of healthy eating, portion control, or sharing, to be demeaning, telling L. Schmidt and other staff, "we're adults," and that this monitoring of portions is akin to treating clients as children. While staff typically attempt to address these concerns respectfully, staff find this constant tension and constant need for monitoring, and constant discontent on the part of clients to be frustrating and this can, in turn, manifest as resistance on the part of staff. One instance that L. Schmidt observed was when an RSA became frustrated when, over the course of one afternoon and night, clients had consumed what was intended to be a four-day supply of cheese. Speaking out of frustration, as all of the RSA's attempts to portion and regulate the cheese had been futile, the RSA said, "well, fine, no more cheese for them!"

Clients are typically receptive of redirection and once they have made their complaint and it has been acknowledged, will allow the subject to drop for the time being. However, clients are more likely to be defensive when staff remind them of their dietary recommendations. In L. Schmidt's observation, clients are more likely to raise their voices or become rude or hateful in their speech when staff draw attention to the disconnect between a client's goal, such as losing weight or managing diabetes through diet, and their actions, such as eating three bowls of ice cream. Lenora shared with L. Schmidt that she had observed one particularly overweight client making two packages of ramen. She told L. Schmidt that she had approached this client and had attempted to respectfully explain to the client the nutritional choices that the client was making, including the high calorie content and high sodium, as this client has talked with both RNs and other staff about her desire to lose weight. Lenora related that the client had gotten very defensive and had raised her voice, repeating "I know, I know," and had given Lenora "the stink eye" for the rest of the day.

This type of response from clients when staff attempt to direct them to healthy choices is typical. Clients will either become defensive and angry or will, as L. Schmidt experienced with one client, attempt to excuse the choice away by talking about how "dark chocolate is good for you," despite being in contradiction with a doctor-recommended diet. Clients are also likely to target those staff who encourage them to make healthy choices by, at a later date, making disparaging comments about that staff's food choices or physical appearance; the female client that Lenora had spoken to later commented to Lenora that it looked as if Lenora was gaining weight.

Staff have emotional responses to these situations and process interactions like this by telling other staff members about them, as Lenora did by telling L. Schmidt and other staff about the client's defensiveness and hostility. This information is important to share from a clinical standpoint as it gives treatment providers an understanding of the client's current mental or emotional state, but sharing also provides the staff member with an opportunity to vent about the situation and to receive validation from peers that they handled the situation appropriately. Staff also discuss unusually unhealthy or bizarre food choices with other staff members. This serves in part to share clinical information but also in part to develop relationships between staff through shared understanding that these food choices are "other," which may serve to validate staff's own food choices. Often these stories are repeated again and again and become part of the folklore of the institution, serving as warnings of what types of behavior or food choices staff should be monitoring.

These retellings are typically humorous in nature and may involve mimicry or animated hand gestures or role-playing. One particular recent favorite is a story Lenora relates of taking two clients to a fast-food restaurant while waiting for a third client to finish at a doctor's appointment. Neither Lenora nor the male client ordered food, but the female client ordered two large hamburgers and a container of ranch dressing. When retelling this story for the benefits of peers, Lenora will play-act eating a hamburger by ripping off a piece of the burger, dipping it in the container of ranch, and eating it, while vividly describing the way in which the piece of burger is drenched and dripping with ranch dressing. Staff typically react with disgust and laughter, though it would be clinically inappropriate and would jeopardize rapport to react in this way to the client herself.

Similarly, staff often find themselves needing to review security footage from the many cameras throughout the building, including that in the kitchen. Sometimes the footage is reviewed specifically because of a food-related question ("who ate eighteen slices of cheese overnight?" or "what happened to the industrial-sized jar of peanut butter?") but more often the footage is being viewed for an unrelated reason; regardless, commenting on client food choices is a common backdrop to reviewing footage. L. Schmidt has participated in many of these interactions. L. Schmidt and other staff will comment upon and joke about client food choices, particularly food choices that seem over-indulgent, such as a gallon of milk, a whole pizza or an entire bunch of bananas. These food choices frustrate staff, but because anger or recrimination is not an appropriate reaction in a treatment setting, staff turn to humor to process and release their emotional responses through jokes and reenactments. These reenactments and retellings serve as a form of catharsis.

Staff and Food

Staff, who may range from licensed clinical social workers to nurses but are most likely to be paraprofessionals (Axer et al., 49), such as Residential Support Assistants (RSAs), are not necessarily trained to navigate food culture or the relationship between a history of trauma or food insecurity and food behavior. In residential settings the emphasis in staff training is on recognizing and intervening appropriately when clients experience behavioral or mental health crises. Little to no attention is paid to the significance of food to clients on an emotional, cultural, or cognitive level, nor to the relationship between a client's food choices and their feelings of control, self-esteem. There is little recognition of clients' ability to assuage emotions related to old trauma linked to food or food insecurity, or to otherwise utilize food as a coping mechanism, or to establish social bonds with peers and/or staff. As Patricia explained, "food is something everybody understands, no matter your clinical understanding. It's common ground ... it can cross professional boundaries." While Patricia suggested this as a means of building rapport with clients, this is also indicative of the personal, rather than professional, approach that staff have toward food and consumption.

This issue is complicated by the fact that many staff struggle with their own relationship to food; care workers are among the most overweight of all workforces, per *The American Journal of Preventive Medicine*. Research supports a strong correlation between binge eating and stress (Harrington et al 214-215). Because staff in residential facilities often work long hours, work split shifts or have schedules that change week to week, staff often find it difficult to maintain a healthy routine of eating at work. Not only are staff schedules unpredictable on a day-to-day basis, but staff in residential facilities also are often interrupted during meal times, and have the added stressor of clients observing and commenting on what a staff member is eating. As already discussed, staff often rely on quick and easy, but high-calorie and low-nutrient fast food or snack foods. Both Carrie and Dana referenced "stress eating" and "eating feelings" when experiencing especially chaotic work or personal environments. These factors contribute to the correlation between care workers and obesity, and inform staff reactions to and interactions with clients in the arena of food.

The majority of staff at the IRTS are women, and women's relationship with food is particularly over-determined by cultural, economic, and social forces. Inthorne and Boyce note, "Women are constantly reminded that their bodies need improvement, with the overweight body, in particular, constructed as deviant" (91). Staff, when asked about their relationships with food, acknowledge that for them, also, food is a complex subject. Many staff struggle with their weight and self-image; as Carrie stated more than once, "I eat my feelings." Patricia acknowledged that weight is a "sensitive subject" for her and recently had a negative experience with clients commenting negatively on her food choices relative to her weight. Lenora related that she struggles with healthy eating and has been "trying to eat better." Dana agreed that maintaining a healthy weight and healthy eating patterns is a "battle." Like Dana, L. Schmidt manages her weight through exercise and mindful eating but finds that such a lifestyle requires significant effort, especially in the context of work-related time

constraints, such as frequent unscheduled overtime, which makes it difficult to maintain a fitness routine, and often leads to missed workouts and
the previously discussed desire to self-reward a difficult or hectic week
with food. When staff joke about, comment upon, or mimic client eating
habits or food choices, these conversations are often accompanied by discussions of staff's own struggles with portion control, healthy eating, or
antagonistic relationship with food. Staff will also swap stories of unusual
foods in their own food culture, often in an attempt to one-up or gross each
other out, such as a recent staff meeting that L. Schmidt attended where
staff described foods eaten in their families, such as pig's feet or coon
jerky, usually to solicit laughter or a disgusted reaction, or described atypical food pairings, such as steak sauce on macaroni and cheese or peanut
butter and pickle sandwiches. By relating their own struggles with food,
staff demonstrate empathy with their clients who share similar difficulties;
continuing to be mindful—a key concept in DBT—of one's own unhealthy
or problematic relationship with foods serves to check judgement of client
food choices that staff may otherwise experience.

Eating is a way that many care workers cope with occupational stress.
As one social worker told us, "We can't get fucked up every night. We
eat our stress." A person who is on call cannot drink or do drugs, but they
can still eat without affecting their ability to respond to a crisis call. Social
critic Caitlin Moran vividly describes this process and the stigma attached:

> Overeating is the addiction of choice of carers, and that's why
> it's come to be regarded as the lowest-ranking of all the addic-
> tions. It's a way of fucking yourself up while still remaining
> fully functional, because you have to. Fat people aren't in-
> dulging in the "luxury" of their addiction making them useless,
> chaotic, or a burden. Instead, they are slowly self-destructing
> in a way that doesn't inconvenience anyone. (Moran)

It appears to be more difficult for staff to detach themselves from their
emotional relationship with food and their own complex relationships,
both positive and negative, with food, body image, family acceptance and
culture, than their potential relationships with other aspects of working in
a psychiatric residential facility. This may be because food culture is so
personal and yet so ubiquitous. In addition, food culture is, within a facility setting, treated much less clinically than mental or behavioral issues.

There are unusually high rates of burnout among the staff who work
most closely with food shopping, preparation, and meal planning, perhaps
because staff, not fully understanding the historical or situational reasons
behind a client's food choices, wish to enforce "good," healthy choices

for clients. As this type of enforcement is not always appropriate in an IRTS, where the focus is on teaching sustainable independent living skills, developing ownership and personal responsibility, and providing person-centered care, staff who are deeply involved in food shopping, preparation, and menu planning become easily burned out because they are aware of the disconnect between a client's stated goals of losing weight, managing diabetes, or being healthy, and their actual behaviors, but do not have the tools to detach themselves from an emotional reaction to this disconnect. When L. Schmidt suggested to Carrie and Patricia, the two staff who have the most food-related responsibilities, that staff who work with food are most likely to get burned out and need to abdicate their responsibilities, both Carrie and Patricia agreed.

Recommendations

Residential facilities may take steps to minimize conflict between staff and clients in the arena of food and may also take steps to minimize burnout among those staff who work most closely in food shopping, preparation, and menu planning.

One way of limiting conflict may be to ensure that clients are aware that staff themselves are not in full control of what foods can be provided and that, in the same way that clients must answer to guardians and/or FCMs, staff must answer to accrediting agencies and DMH. This acknowledgement of limited control on the part of both clients and staff may serve to alleviate or distract from the power differential and permit a less confrontational relationship between clients and staff.

Staff have noted that the self-destructive or otherwise unhealthy relationships with food tend to be correlated with a lack of other activities and interests. As Patricia expressed it, "people with outside interests, like jobs, maybe get joy or pleasure" from those activities, whereas those clients whom staff find the most conflictual to interact with are those who have the most limited outside interests—those without jobs, natural supports such as family, friends or relationships outside of the residential facility and who have fewer diversions. Eating may substitute for these other activities as a source of interest or fulfillment. Patricia noted, "a lot of it is out of boredom. When they're bored, they eat. I've seen people go get bowls of ice cream or whole other meals because they have nothing else to do." Often clients with limited work, hobbies, or leisure activities are those who are most likely to consistently overeat. Staff could work more closely to assist these clients in developing outside interests and increase their social ties, which may reduce clients' desires to be conflictive and controlling regarding their food, as by developing these other interests or hobbies clients will increase the areas of their lives over which they do have control and assist clients in developing a sense of gratification or accomplishment unrelated to food. Food may also then no longer be the primary arena of control in their lives.

Facilities and institutions may also reduce tension between and among clients and staff and burnout among staff by giving client relationships with food the attention that this complex subject deserves; this is an under-discussed and under-studied area in residential facilities, and yet client relationships with food cannot be separated from their mental, emotional, or behavioral health and all areas must be addressed holistically and using a person-centered methodology. One way of doing this would be to assist staff in bringing a clinical understanding to their interactions with and reactions to clients regarding clients' attitudes toward food and their food choices. Staff are taught to be detached and professional when dealing with mental or behavioral health issues, such as not validating delusional thinking, de-escalating verbal aggression, or assisting clients in coping with symptoms of anxiety or depression, but they are not taught to bring clinical skills to bear in de-escalating conflict relating to food. Nor are they trained to utilize clinical techniques, such as the Dialectical Behavioral Therapy (DBT) skill "wise mind," which emphasizes a non-judgmental attitude and assists practitioners in recognizing and discarding cognitive distortion. Nor yet do they learn to adopt the person-centered approach, a key value in many mental health agencies, recognizing that each individual is in a different place in their wellness and recovery. Staff are familiar with and use these skills in relation to mental illness, but because food traditionally falls under a personal rather than professional purview, these skills do not inform staff interaction and reaction relating to food. However, staff may use "wise mind" and mindfulness inherent in DBT teachings to respond in an empathetic and non-judgmental way to client food choices that may otherwise lead to frustration among the staff and an increased feeling of resentment or resistance among clients.

Currently little attention is paid to the complex relationships that clients have with food. As already discussed, a client's relationship with food may be related to a history of trauma, homelessness or food insecurity, may be used as a coping tool in lieu of healthier coping skills, and may serve as a substitute for other interests and sources of fulfillment or empowerment. Staff must be educated on these convoluted relationships and taught to bring the same clinical detachment to food issues as to mental health and behavioral issues. Staff would benefit from having regular training to minimize the personal baggage that they bring to their place of work; as already discussed, staff, as well as clients, struggle with complex cultural and personal relationships with food, just as many staff have experience with substance abuse or mental illness among their own family or friends. The difference is that staff understand substance abuse and mental health from a professional, clinical perspective while the same cannot be said for relationships with food. Consulting with folklorists who specialize in foodways and food culture can give training staff the tools to build and share an understanding of food that encompasses trauma, medicine, culture, and identity.

Strikingly, the staff who work most closely with clients in the arena of food are those who are least equipped to be clinical in their interactions with and reactions to clients and their food choices, and most likely to react with intolerance or frustration to the conflictual attitudes that clients bring to the arena of food; it is the paraprofessionals, the residential support staff, who work most closely with clients in preparing food and who are responsible for grocery shopping and menu planning. Yet these are the staff that receive the least professional training. Typically, RSA staff receive brief, general trainings on a monthly or even less frequent basis, while the clinical treatment staff have more frequent access to lengthy conferences and multi-day trainings on clinical strategies that assist staff in developing and maintaining healthy boundaries, emotional wellbeing, and to separate personal biases from professional performance, all necessary to avoid burnout and to maintain therapeutic client-staff interactions. The paraprofessional staff would benefit from this same level of training. Indeed, all staff would benefit from frequent on-the-job trainings to remind themselves of clinical treatment concepts and to minimize burnout through the validation of the value of their profession and contributions.

Conclusions

It is easier for workers to be clinical in regard to issues that are more obviously mental health-related, such as hearing voices, delusions, self-harm, lying, manipulation, and aggression than for workers to be clinical when it comes to food choices. At the same time, workers' own food issues can exacerbate food-related conflict and client resistance and resentment. As Melvyn Rose notes, "Clarity about our own motivations might help us find the way to circumvent their inevitable compulsion to reject" (Rose 155). As Smith has observed, social workers' decision-making can be understood as dependent on the culture of the institution and is often self-described as "instinct." The decision-making used by workers draws on clinical training that seeks to minimize mirroring the emotional and impulsive behavior of clients (Smith 437) but must be appropriate to the culture of the institution or agency in order to be effective. Forkby and Höjer argue that social work decisions are often based in collective memory, oral narrative, and "gut" responses (166). Food is intimately related to the gut; decisions about food are always complicated because food is tied to individual and cultural identity but mediated by larger discourses of health, beauty, and morality. Thus, how to respond to food-related conflict is a heavily freighted decision for workers.

Helping workers be more clinical in their approach to their clients' interactions with food may help workers learn to intervene to de-escalate potential conflict between clients. Use of techniques such as the skills already discussed may not only allow staff to approach clients' food choices from a clinical, rather than a personal, standpoint in order to minimize conflict, maintain client rapport, and reduce burnout among staff but, if taught to clients themselves in relation to their food choices and emotional connection to food, may also serve to help clients identify and understand the motivations behind their food choices and ultimately reframe their relationship with food.

Folklorists can help care workers bridge the gap between personal and professional, gut reaction and clinically-informed decision-making. Public folklore and public health can, as Michael Owen Jones suggests, work together to build a stronger, more culturally informed understanding of the relationship between food, health, belief, and morality. While on the national level, public folklore such as the 2005 Smithsonian Institution's Festival of American Folklife has had an increased focus on food, public folklorists in the state of Missouri have the opportunity to make foodways a much more pronounced part of their programming in festivals, arts apprenticeships, websites, and outreach and education. The Missouri Folk Arts Program has emphasized the relationship between Missouri sustainable agriculture and Missouri food culture, and has supported traditional arts apprenticeships in foodways (such as Ozark home hog butchering). As Long observes, food is an important way that folklore concepts can be introduced to the public (4). As we have demonstrated in this article, giving foodways the attention it deserves can have wide-reaching impacts for all Missourians.

Works Cited

Axer, Andrzej, Michael Donohue, David Moore, and Tom Welch. "Training and Supervision of Residential Staff in Community-based Treatment Facilities." *Archives of Psychiatry and Psychotherapy* 3 (2013): 49-56.

Ben-Amos, Dan. "Toward a Definition of Folklore in Context." *Toward New Perspectives in Folklore* eds. Americo Paredes and Richard Bauman. Bloomington, IN: Trickster Press, 1972.

Brewerton, Timothy D. "Posttraumatic Stress Disorder and Disordered Eating: Food Addiction as Self-Medication." *Journal of Women's Health* 20.8 (2011): 1133-1134.

Coffey, Michael. "Resistance and Challenge: Competing Accounts in Aftercare Monitoring." *Sociology of Health and Illness* 33.5 (2011) 748-760.

Cross, Maria. "History of Prison Food." *Prison Service Journal* 185 (2009): 21-27.

Counihan, Carole M. *The Anthropology of Food and the Body: Gender, Meaning, and Power*. New York: Routledge, 2009.

Delaney, Mary and Mary B. McCarthy. "Saints, Sinners and Non-Believers: the Moral Space of Food. A Qualitative Exploration of Beliefs and Perspectives on Healthy Eating of Irish Adults Aged 50–70." *Appetite* 73 (2014): 105-113.

Doudna, Kimberly D., Angelica S. Reina, and Kimberly "Longitudinal Associations Among Food Insecurity, Depressive Symptoms, and Parenting." *Journal of Rural Mental Health* 39.3-4 (2015): 178-187.

Earle, Rod and Coretta Phillips. "Digesting Men? Ethnicity, Gender, and Food: Perspectives from a 'Prison Ethnography.'" *Theoretical Criminology* 16.2 (2012): 141-156.

Everett, Holly. "Vernacular Health Moralities and Culinary Tourism in Newfoundland and Labrador." *The Journal of American Folklore* 122.-483 (2009): 28-52.

Forkby, Torbjörn and Staffan Höjer. "Navigations Between Regulations and Gut Instinct: the Unveiling of Collective Memory in Decision-making Processes Where Teenagers are Placed in Residential Care." *Child and Family Social Work* 16 (2011): 159-168.

Godderis, Rebecca. "Dining In: The Symbolic Power of Food in Prison." *The Howard Journal* 45.3(2006): 255-267.

Harrington, Ellen F., Janis H. Crowther, Heather C. Payne Henrickson, and Kristen D. Mickelson. "The Relationships among Trauma, Stress, Ethnicity, and Binge Eating." *Cultural Diversity and Ethnic Minority Psychology* 12.2 (2006): 212-229.

Inthorn, Sanna and Tammy Boyce. "It's Disgusting How Much Salt You Eat!: Television Discourses of Obesity, Health, and Morality." *The International Journal of Cultural Studies* 13.1 (2010): 83-100.

Jones, Michael Owen. "Eating Behind Bars: Prison Pruno, Spreads, and the Suicide Loaf." American Folklore Society 2012 Annual Meeting.

New Orleans: American Folklore Society 25 October, 2012.

——. "Food Choice, Symbolism, and Identity: Bread-and-Butter Issues for Folkloristics and Nutrition Studies." *Journal of American Folklore* 120.476 (2007): 129-177.

Lawrence, Shawn A., Rebekah Hazlett & Eileen Mazur Abel. "Obesity Related Stigma as a Form of Oppression: Implications for Social Work Education." *Social Work Education* 31.1 (2012): 63-74.

Long, Lucy M. "Introduction, Special Issue: Food and Identity in the Americas." *Journal of American Folklore* 122.483 (2009) 3-10.

Luckhaupt, Sara E. et al. "Prevalence of Obesity Among U.S. Workers and Associations with Occupational Factors." *American Journal of Preventive Medicine* 46.3 (2014): 237 - 248

Mishna, Faye, Barbara Muskat, and Gerald Schamass. "Food for Thought: The Use of Food in Group Therapy with Children and Adolescents." *The International Journal of Group Psychotherapy* 52.1 (2002): 27-47.

Moran, Caitlin. *How to Be a Woman.* New York: Harper Perennial, 2011.

Muldoon, Katherine A., Putu K. Duff, Sarah Fielden, and Aranka Anema. "Food Insufficiency is Associated with Psychiatric Morbidity in a Nationally Representative Study of Mental Illness Among Food Insecure Canadians." *Social Psychiatry and Psychiatric Epidemiology* 48 (2013): 795-803.

Perelman, Deb. *Smitten Kitchen.* Smittenkitchen.com.

Peterman, Jerusha Nelson, Parke E. Wilde, Sidney Liang, Odelia I. Bermudez, Linda Silka, and Beatrice Lorge Rogers. "Relationship Between Past Food Deprivation and Current Dietary Practices and Weight Status Among Cambodian Refugee Women in Lowell, MA." *Research & Practice: American Journal of Public Health* 100.10 (2010): 1930-1937.

Roberts, Seren Haf and Jois Elisabeth Bailey. "Incentives and Barriers to Lifestyle Interventions for People with Severe Mental Illness: a Narrative Synthesis of Quantitative, Qualitative and Mixed Methods Studies." *Journal of Advanced Nursing* (2011): 690-708.

Rose, Melvyn. "The Function of Food in Residential Treatment." *The Journal of Adolescence* 10.2 (1987): 149-162.

Smith, Yvonne. "Rethinking Decision-Making: An Ethnographic Study of Worker Agency in Crisis Intervention." *Social Service Review* 88.3 (2014): 407-442.

Smoyer, Amy B. "Good and Healthy: Foodways and Construction of Identity in a Women's Prison." *The Howard Journal of Criminal Justice* 53.5 (2014): 525-541.

Smoyer, Amy B. "Making Fatty Girl Cakes: Food and Resistance in a

Women's Prison." *The Prison Journal* 96.2 (2016): 191-209.

Spiegel, Alison. "The 22 Most Hipster Foods on the Planet." *The Huffington Post* 15 April, 2014.

Taylor, Valerie H., Robert S. McIntyre, Gary Remington, Robert Levitan, Brian Stonehocker, and Arya M. Sharma. "Beyond Pharmacotherapy: Understanding the Links Between Obesity and Chronic Mental Illness." *Canadian Journal of Psychiatry* 57.1 (2012): 5-12.

Ugelvik, Thomas. "The Hidden Food: Mealtime Resistance and Identity Work in a Norwegian Prison." *Punishment and Society* 13.1 (2011): 47-63.

The Politics of Transference in Traditional Fiddling: A Narrative Case Study (Willi Goehring)

I was driving down a one-lane highway, about an hour east of my home in Fayetteville, Arkansas. It was early October of 2012, I was twenty-three, and the trees had begun to dazzle the low, granite bluffs with their fall colors. There was a slight rain, and the fog that lingered on the hills made them more than a bit forbidding. My '88 Ford struggled and heaved. I pulled up outside the Ozark Clayworks, near Osage—an old General Store. All the clay and stoneware there were made by hand, using methods both prehistoric and new-age, and I imagined I would feel like a king drinking from any of the coffee cups, two of which I bought. I could tell the floors themselves were several generations old, and I ended up in a long conversation with the store-owner, who had plied her trade there for forty years. I mentioned, by and by, that I was in the area here to meet an old fiddler, to find my way up the mountain to meet him, record him, learn tunes, and she said, "oh, I know Billy." I would later learn that the scale where Billy weighed each of his newborn children was only a few feet away on the floor of that shop. I would learn a lot of things that seemed wild to me during my visits with Billy Matthews, Ozark fiddler, banjoist, and builder.

From the clayworks, it was a fifteen minute climb up a steep unmarked road that began paved, became gravel, then dirt, then no road at all, a ramble punctuated by a steep climb on nearly green grass, following the tire-marks. A decrepit cinder-block structure lay to the east. This, I would learn, was the workshop where Billy used to build banjos, but now it's full of rats, full of black mold. Then there was Shady Grove, the abandoned church with its graveyard and some of Osage's oldest inhabitants. Billy used to send his children there when he and his wife wanted to make whoopie, and the kids would climb down the mountain and break into the creaky church, shinnying up to the top of the steeple to ring its bell. That's how the adults would know the kids were coming back home, and they'd have supper on by the time the kids got back up the bluff. These were the sorts of places I was canceling my classes at the University of Arkansas to go see, the sort of stories that made a pile of hundreds of Composition-101 papers composed on the same subject seem infinitely more inert than the squawk and bustle of an oldtime stringband. I felt positively Lomaxian, like Mary Celestia Parler in her army jeep, going out to meet contacts, learn songs and stories and culture.

My poor truck sputtered, shook, and trundled along a path into a clearing where the house Billy built himself still stands. He was sitting on the porch, and friends visiting from Illinois and Missouri were making small repairs to the porch that was almost completely separated from the old house, battered by time and the elements. He built the whole homestead with salvaged goods, stolen goods, repurposed ones, and raised his family there. It has an area that "the raccoons own." Billy was sitting smoking a cigarette. He had very recently nearly died from smoking related illnesses, so I was nervous just to meet him again, and we shook hands and had small talk. I felt like a jerk for not helping with the repair projects, like the helpless Yankee transplant that I was, unhandy with both a hammer and fiddle. But his friends, Christine, Paul, and Suzi, were so delightful and welcoming I nearly forgot another small shame: that I hadn't brought a damn thing, no little tribute to honor my outsider status. No beer, no food, no smokes. I felt like a guest. But we drank beer, smoked, and by and by we convinced Billy that we should play some tunes. I drug my fiddle from my truck and we set up chairs in the kitchen just as the cicadas were beginning to churn in the humidity.

I first heard of Billy from the internet, during the countless Google searches for "Ozark Traditional Music" and "Ozark History" I made from my urban apartment complex after I arrived in Arkansas for graduate school. "Fiddlin' Banjo Billy Matthews," as his website described him, was a true keeper of the flame, and had a project of some 500 fiddle tunes, known and obscure, you could purchase in a 5 CD set. Because I was used to using databases, archives, and begging, borrowing, and especially stealing my antique music collection (the 60's era Harry Smith Anthology has disappeared from more than one public library because of teenage ne'er-do-wells like myself) I have yet to buy any of Billy's music, but have listened to and recorded countless hours. Then, during my first year of fiddling, jamming at a local bar, attending square dances, cake-walks, and house-parties, I talked my way into a cheap ride to Clifftop, WV, the largest festival gathering of oldtime musicians in the world.

Caption: Billy's Homestead. Photo by Suzi Vause.

Once there, I happened across Billy's friends, Christine and Suzi. We had a few somewhat obscure Ozark tunes in common—"Finley Creek Blues" (after Kirkwood, Missouri's Vesta Johnson) and "9th of January" (after Ava, Missouri's Bob Holt), and this was strange enough, halfway across the country, that we got to talking. The next day, Suzi and Christine told me, and I quote: "We think you're the next big thing in oldtime music."

I remember my ego stammered as the festivals' several thousand old-time musicians were burning through the twisty annals of old tunes. If a bomb had gone off at Clifftop, hundreds of traditional melodies might've died entirely, and I was the torchbearer of literally none. But I admit, it was something an obsessed person wanted to hear. They explained they were looking for someone who might be willing to be taught by a master, who might stick with it, and who would acknowledge the master when he played the tunes. This is, of course, the model for oldtime music appren-ticeship. "I learned this from" is the respectful preamble to any tune. I accepted the offer, we played for a half-an-hour, I learned one tune, and we all tomcatted away into the night.

In that first circle at Billy's homestead, we tuned up, and started in the key of G. He started with a tune he learned from Jimmy Wheeler, "Goin'

Back to Old Kentucky." "What's that guy's name?" Billy said over and over again, scratching his bald head. The folks asked if I'd like to sit right next to Billy, and I declined, saying "I'm not sure how much that'll help anything." Billy: "it's sort of like half a tune with its repeating phrases." We moved on to another tune that did that too, "Nellie Grey," of Civil War fame. This was the progression throughout our evening and many others: swilling beer, talking shop, free-associating from Billy's enormous vocabulary of music. It could take him as many as five minutes to remember how a tune went— sometimes he would even play the wrong one to try to call a similar one back to his fingers. "Magpie" "Shoes and Stockings," "Chasing the Federals," "The Muskattatuck" waltz. So on, ad infinitum, until the man petered out. I tried to keep up, but mostly listened. By the last iteration of a tune, I might've sawed a few notes along with everyone.

Billy's mental and CD-format collection of 500 fiddle tunes is a teaching object, a piece of oral literature. It has tunes older than the Civil War and easily entrenched in our vernacular, and others as obscure and foreign to the ear as anything: polkas, cakewalks, rags, mazurkas, tunes delicate and indelicate, waltzes and airs, ditties and sentimental ballads and particularly schottisches, his bow rockings and chord shapings eloquently parsing what is often played as a vaguely Scottish stumble.

Billy's style is generally one of overstatement, one that doesn't attach perfect nuance or nostalgia to individual tunes in the style of any one person but himself. The pace Billy plays at is unharried, and generally just below square dance speed. He enjoys using chords' shapes, often slides into third position to find his note, and generally avoids florid bowing patterns that involve multiple upstrokes. This is true of most Ozark fiddlers. Billy has a great sense of rhythm, and truncates his saw-strokes and bow-rocks with an idiosyncrasy more charming than it is distracting: small pauses and staccato phrasings. If one were to ignore the accomplishment represented by his enormous repertoire, he would still be an above-average Ozark-style fiddler with an extremely listenable and danceable style. It was difficult, if not impossible, to fall into step with the romance of his playing while in his house. Especially when the moonshine was doled out by the thimbleful—there was precious little left of it. Just enough to savor the burn.

There were, of course, other oldtime fiddlers I was studying with— Billy's old band, The Skirtlifters, had several members I could reasonably have claimed to be apprenticing under. At the very least, they were people who I either constantly bothered or constantly tried to bother. Curly Miller (of The Old 78's) gave me some tenor banjo sheet music only months before his cancer took him. I learned tunes from Jim Lansford's recordings shortly before he died. I get drunk and play and call square dances with the rest of them to this day.

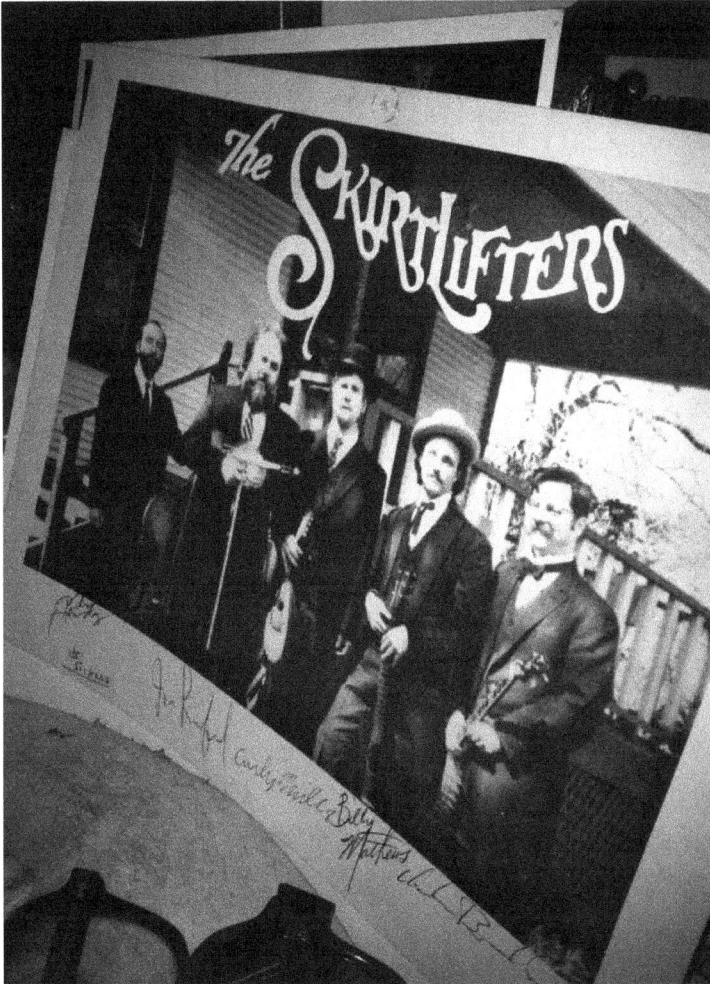

Caption: *A print from the heyday of the Skirtlifters. Left to Right: Pete Howard, Jim Lansford, Curly Miller, Billy Matthews, Clarke Buehling. Photo by Suzi Vause.*

But at the time of my first visit to Billy Matthews' homestead in 2012 I was desperate for apprenticeship and fellowship, to feel like an insider to the culture that I was beginning to love, but didn't have a way into. I was a collector of old music who couldn't play. But when I stumbled upon some old recordings of Carl Sandburg several years prior, his singing made me think, "hey, I could do this!" I was trying on an accent, trying on a music, trying on a home to honor my obsession, a suburban boy spending hours with his shadow draped over a fiddle in a squalid apartment complex, shirking most responsibilities an adjunct instructor of English has —not grading, showing up late to teach in flannels and overalls, bringing a fiddle into class, giving impromptu lessons on Ozark flora and fauna. I was even putting square dances into my calendar a whole year in advance, despite being so depressed I sometimes didn't know if I was going to make it all the way to the last dance of the year. When someone told me they thought I was talented (as opposed to a carpetbagging whippersnapper), my heart stood at attention.

Because it was an impressive and powerful cultural idea, knowing and playing 500 tunes. Folklorist Alan Jabbour said of his major subject Henry Reed (1884-1968) of West Virginia, from whom he collected around 200 fiddle tunes:

> "[Henry Reed] was a kind of musical encyclopedia of his region and era, and virtually every musical influence that lingered from yore or wafted by from the world about him seems to have been imprinted in his imagination. To scan his repertory is to abandon forever both the notion that the Appalachian region was culturally isolated a hundred years ago, and the notion that ancient traditions are best preserved when there is no contact with the new. His tunes reveal splendidly both the depth and grandeur of the older fiddling tradition of the nineteenth-century frontier, and the richly textured fabric of continuing musical creativity in the region throughout the first half of the twentieth century."

Billy Matthew's 500 tunes, variously remembered, repaired, and altered, have a lot in common with the 19th century inheritances of Henry Reed. Both men were attracted to a great variety of tune types: breakdowns, rags, pop songs, squirrely little modal pieces, and so on. Billy's repertoire, his commitment to its memory, and his personal style, all bring up the same particular romance: the depth and grandeur, the textured fabric, the cultural inheritance that leads us to understand place and time holistically. Billy will note, though, that he has no particular affinity toward region with the possible exception he avoids the Appalachian region's typical Scots-Irish-style tunes (perhaps over-represented in contemporary oldtime music) and popular tunes in favor of the German/Swedish midwestern diaspora, as well as Ozark variations of classic tunes (perhaps under-represented). As with Henry Reed, though, his performances of these tunes are a part of oral transmission, a piece of culture gleaned entirely by ear from living people.

Unlike Henry Reed, though, Billy was born and raised in the suburbs of a Northern state, and fell in love with oldtime music as a revivalist in the 60's and 70's, where, for a brief time (it is rumored) he knew Bob Dylan and other prominent members of the folk revival, who were involved in politicizing, and, by some accounts, colonizing American vernacular music. These and other revivalists were cracking the code to the 'heritage' learning model, the product and transmission of embodied, local knowledges, in order to claim some small amount of participation in American heritage, warts and all. The Ozarks, with tourist cities like Branson, Mountain View, Hot Springs and Eureka Springs, as well as exceptionally cheap land, were ripe for back-to-the-landers with a penchant for performing. And thus, as with Henry Reed's huge contribution to our understanding of American vernacular music, Billy Matthews has contributed vastly and variously to the revival of it.

Sitting in his kitchen, playing tunes learned from a lifetime in oldtime music, the contrast between revivalism and thing-revived was striking. Instead of being like a Lomax, I was visiting a site of re-enactment on a very deep level. Outside of the usual heritage model of transmission (local-to-local, father-to-son), Billy had created the life of a hillbilly largely by following his instincts towards the music, seeking apprenticeship and practicing doggedly in a self-induced microcosm. His sagging, out-of-the-way house, his choice to build banjos and play music for a living, his choice to have home-births and subsistence agriculture, and so on, were all a part of a revivalism of a culture that, while not yet dead, has been diminishing for hundreds of years. It was as much hippy-dom as it was hillbilly-dom, as much nerdy history as fanatic self-reliance.

But what of this huge, varied repertory, bigger than most fiddlers possess? What about years of going to festivals, playing gigs, jamming, learning from archives and living history? It struck me then that Billy is a *living embodiment* of the American old-time fiddler's repertory almost as much as any one person could be. True to form, some of the tunes are fragmentary, some of them are unfinished, and some, even, were learned in the "wrong key" according to their original sources.

Caption: *Billy in his kitchen, resting between tunes. Photo by Suzi Vause.*

So, unlike the note-for-note learner, the diligent student, and the blue-grasser, the narrative behind each of those tunes is Billy's own, not one that lives in an archive or piece of hoardable culture. It is a repertoire that plots actual scenarios that are not mimetic, or copies, or revivals, but exist independently in time and space as a way of knowing. By the third day of sitting in a circle of chairs in Billy's house, listening to him pontificate and then recall, forget, and then discuss again in between his arpeggiations, I realized: this isn't only music, this is an argument about how to live in the world. We became, in his kitchen, no more self-aware than Henry Reed was. We were playing our music, with each other, talking about the people we learned it from, honored ghosts and dear friends.

I swelled to Lomaxian proportions again, or perhaps only to the size my fourth or fifth beer would've allowed. "Prairie du Rocher Motion," "Rick-ett's Hornpipe," "Fat Meat and Dumplings" roared on. Unlike pop fiddling (bluegrass, swing, country), where nuance and regional variety are sup-planted by the immediate needs of culture, this was the vernacular social music of the continent. We crossed state lines, and found them useful to delineate styles. This stuff was surviving, mostly unaltered, not because of money, but because of the value it had beyond money— a renegade thing, like home-grown tomatoes one family can harvest and share. While Dolly Parton's show raged just an hour northwards in Branson, this was a performance that momentarily clogged the machine of post-industrial capitalism: everything in person, everything by ear, everything "better than it sounds," everything in the ever-dissipating live moment.[1]

Which is to say, the fiddle tune, when experienced this way, is a sort of cultural ground-zero, enacting the friction that Derrida describes between an event and citation. Without citation, he tells us, there can be no speech act. Without a signified mnemonic, there can be no episteme.[2] The citation in oldtime music relies upon the mistake, slip-up, and misnomer: it dignifies the imprecision of the old, shaky hands of masters who might have had demonstration only once or twice from their own masters. It is both local and national. Pan-american tune-families have their local episteme where "Turkey in the Straw" is "Natches Under the Hill" a few miles westward, and "John Brown's Hangin' from a Sour Apple Tree" in North Carolina is "Battle Hymn of the Republic" elsewhere. These citations use personal idiosyncrasy and local styles in hyper-conservative microcosms where the phrase: "I learned this from" could begin a patrilineal (and occasionally matrilineal) digression that digs further into local, social history than almost any other craft. For, unlike bodging, quilting, or potting, music is first and foremost a social activity that brings people together to dance, court, touch. The mnemonics generate a localized epistemology that can represent a person, time, or place broadly. The oldtime fiddle tune is metonymy for a whole swath of pre-industrial oral culture that finds its home in the archive of the human mind. In Billy's house, then, we were investigating disparate and multiple historical moments in order to consider past, present, and future in varied patterns, figures, and flourishes.

These are large shoes to fill. For revivalists, there is a complex relationship between citation and event because the citation is often (but not always) of a dead man from a place we have never been. Archives, online info-dumps, race records, and vast collections of digital music make easy narratives out of these, and it is in these narratives that the dingy stereotypes of blues legends and bucktoothed yahoos survive and are perpetuated. If you are Billy Matthews, you settle this comic eulogizing of the backwards and impoverished dead by moving to a place where the

---

[1]These are concepts broadly from Diana Taylor's great book *The Archive and the Repertoire: Performing Cultural Memory in the Americas* and Peggy Phelan's article "The Ends of Performance."

[2]This I borrow from Derrida's *Signature, Event, Context.*

people continue to live, and live yourself in the culture and community, emigrating from self-aware emulation in folk clubs to the self-evident creation and consumption of a highly self-reliant culture. In a post-industrial society dominated by archive (where any living body of knowledge is on the brink of utter digitization), championing the embodied and unwritten oral-expression feels intuitive, if primitivist.

Especially when it leads to dancing, to touching, to the things a young man yearns for. The performances at Billy's homestead were, he said "too slow, 'cause nobody's dancing," but during much of our time together the result of our efforts was absolutely evident: a room full of pattering feet, rowdiness, sweat, fists, kisses, and the poetry of the square-dance caller. What could be called pretentious about our learning together always comes under an assault of drunken laughter from young and old alike, people who are making meaningful connections and lifelong friendships at our bi-monthly hootenannies. While I was, for a time, still too depressed to choose anything for myself but which television show to rewatch and which fast food to order, these earnest and self-sustaining cultural performances were becoming absolutely normative, discursive, and unsubjective forces for good in my life. What I sought after like a wealthy colonialist looking for savage, ancient music was becoming a part of my bones. I kept noticing when I was being pretentious, when I was talking too much and listening too little. I became humbled and participatory, and I hope I remain that way.

Caption: Author and Billy Matthews at Billy's homestead. Photo by Suzi Vause.

While I fell asleep that first night at Billy's place, warned with stories (all improbable) about cougars and wild hogs, I kept thinking I was living in some sort of dream. But I wasn't; I awoke to the whir of chainsaws and the clatter of tools as Billy's friends and apprentices cut firewood and fixed his truck like good neighbors. Like a dreamer and an academic, I kept my eyes closed until the late hours of the morning, still unable to lift a finger and prove my absolute imprecision with a hammer. I didn't know if I could be a part of the place I loved or not.

The second time we met, I saw Billy win a lifetime achievement award as a Master of Ozark Fiddling, in addition to first prize in the senior division of the Arkansas Fiddle Contest. I was delighted and saw the playing of old-timers who would die in just a few years, including Ray Curbow, the "barefoot fiddler" of Blue Eye, Missouri. The audience was perhaps thirty. So what exactly is the purpose of Billy's project? It's his profession—he makes his living from CD sales, lessons, and workshops—but he is certainly not the finest fiddler I know (better dance fiddlers abound, and he often requires two or three takes to get certain passages correct among the hundreds of tunes he remembers), nor the most regionally-sourced (some locals come to mind who were born and raised here, learned from grandparents who learned from their grandparents), nor the most commercially viable (superstars like Chris Thile and Bela Fleck move back and forth effortlessly between Bach and terrible oldtime classics like "Cluck Old Hen" or "Bile Them Cabbage," making tons).

What Billy does have is a maximal, extensive repertoire in extremis and in the very location that an archive is usually located. He is himself an archive. He has listened, he has heard, and is bearing witness with work that has gathered little dust over the years. Like many unmonied people, myself among them, Billy cannot take very good care of himself. He will die, as all fiddlers do, and possibly without a lot of recognition for his work. Yet his impact is wider than most, and indelible in me.

Fours years later, a week before writing this piece, I was sitting with Owen Rein, chairmaker and carpenter, of Stone County, Arkansas, and Arkansas Living Treasure Award nominee (though he told me he was tired of being involved with the award after more than one nomination). He's been working from his homestead for nearly thirty years, making chairs in the Shaker style, and has a deeply ecological view of his craft, his land, his labor. He said something that made me think of Billy. It was: "There were quite a few back-to-the-landers [in the Ozarks]...where you can have a choice on your home economics. How you spend your money, your lifestyle ... how to make the numbers work in your favor. If there's one thing humans can do, it's be flexible. We can live anywhere. An igloo, a car, a penthouse ... sometimes we choose to live in a new way for no reason at all, just because we want a change."

Where can wisdom and authenticity be found? Can forty years of dogged self-reliance and self-education make a true hillbilly? Four years later, I can say I don't care. In the long run, it's the tunes I care about, the people I've danced with, the visits we've had and will continue to have. In a world where *Duck Dynasty* expresses the rural idiom to the public perhaps more than any other single entity, I take comfort that somewhere Billy Mathews is tucked into the life he hewed and lashed together, with no internet, no Facebook, no TV, and a phone only at the desperate urgings of his friends. I'm comforted that no matter what I say about authenticity, about revivalism, no matter how I speculate on how to live a good life in a confusing world, that somewhere Billy Mathews, Ozark Fiddler, is pulling his bow across a rosin cake.

Works Cited

Derrida, Jacques, and Barry Stocker. *Jacques Derrida: Basic Writings*. Introduction. London: Routledge, 2007. Print.

Diehl, Heath A., Peggy Phelan, and Jill Lane. "The Ends of Performance." *The Journal of the Midwest Modern Language Association* 34.3 (2001): 94-95. Web.

Jabbour, Alan. "Henry Reed: His Life, His Influence, His Art." Library of Congress. Web. 09 Aug. 2016.

Taylor, Diana. *The Archive and the Repertoire: Performing Cultural Memory in the Americas*. Durham: Duke UP, 2003. Print.

Reflections on Public Folk Arts from a Traditional Artist
By
Gladys Caines Coggswell

Finding Frankford; Finding a Home

I fell in love with the state of Missouri, and I now call it my home. Missouri welcomed me with open arms. My first visit to Frankford, Missouri was out of curiosity. While my former husband Truman and I were driving south on Highway 61 from Hannibal, we saw the sign: Frankford. We had never heard of Frankford and genuinely wanted to find out more about it. As we entered town, a second sign informed us that Frankford's population was 356 people. We parked on Main Street in front of the Daisy Patch, a craft shop where folks gathered to drink coffee, learn to produce some sort of craft, and catch up on their neighbors' lives. When I stepped out of the car, I was immediately overcome by a magical, spiritual, and emotional sensation. I felt as if that wasn't my first time to visit Frankford. I am originally from New Jersey, but Frankford felt like home, and I never experienced this feeling before nor since. Prior to that day, Truman and I lived in Doniphan, Mo., in Ripley County near the Arkansas border and then in St. Louis, for a total of seven years. In fact, we were driving around the area looking for a home to purchase.

131

Gladys Coggswell. (Photo by Alex W. Barker)

We went inside the Daisy Patch and there was Mrs. Millie Reading, a warm, friendly woman who wholeheartedly welcomed us to Frankford. She was the owner and talented instructor of arts at the Daisy Patch. We stayed and talked for over an hour. I was sad when it was time to go. I loved Frankford, and I knew we were going to move there. About three months went by, and we did. I was enamored with this quaint little town. After we purchased a home there, it occurred to me that I had such a good time that I didn't once think about race. I was surprised to learn that there were only six black people there. Mrs. Reading was white, and when we met it felt as if we were old friends. Our instant friendship transcended the color of our skin.

We were anxious to visit the African American Second Christian Church of Frankford. When we did, there were only three other black people there. Mrs. Camie Doolin was the Sunday school teacher, pianist, and she preached. It was difficult to get a preacher for three or four listeners. She must have been in her eighties, and she was very nice but very stern. You couldn't be one minute late or chew gum during the service. She had some good things to say, and some not so good things to say about Frankford. She wasn't going anywhere though because Mrs. Doolin had work to do, and according to her "nobody else could do it." She had been a leader in the Second Christian Church of Frankford most of her life. It was she who made sure that racial rights were addressed.

One day she told me that her brother was run out of Frankford, and he never came back. She didn't go into detail about that, but she seemed annoyed when she mentioned it. She told me some of the history of the house that Truman and I bought. Mr. Garrison Gardner, a "free man of color," bought the property around 1856, nine years before the end of the Civil War. Mr. Garrison was a successful shoemaker and church member. He couldn't read or write because the laws forbade schooling for blacks at the time. But he could count his money right, and he knew the Bible because his daughter read to him daily, and he memorized the scriptures. Mr. Garrison became a respected man of Frankford and a prominent shoe-maker. He sold the property to another "free man of color" in 1865 for a profit.

Mrs. Marie Campbell, another black resident, was responsible for the upkeep of the black cemetery and the two black churches (the other church is the African Methodist Episcopal "AME" Church). She invited me to Choir Day, a tradition that takes place on the first Sunday of every May. It is an event that takes place in many of Missouri's black communities annually. Mrs. Campbell was in her mid-sixties when I met her. She always cooked luscious dishes for the Frankford Choir Day, and people brought gospel songs and empty stomachs. There was always more than enough of that scrumptious food. People who had once lived in Frankford or in the area would come home. Many still had relatives living near there. They would sing gospel, meet and greet old friends, and eat. It was just like a scene from a family reunion. The church was small, but it was packed. When the Second Christian Church became a safety hazard, Choir Day took place in the old black AME Church. I was told that the church was built by the hands of the town's black men in the 1800's. There was never enough room in the little hot church for all of the people who came on Choir Day. Many would have to stand outside to listen to the choirs. The celebration would last for up to five hours. Money collected was to pay for the cemetery and church's upkeep expenses. It was hard to believe that there were once enough black people living in Frankford to support two churches.

Mrs. Vivian South, another black senior citizen of Frankford, told me a very sad story about two local little boys. She said that one was a black boy and the other was white. As young children, they played together and spent weekends together. On the morning they started elementary school, they were excited about going to kindergarten. When their mothers reached the top of the hill, the boys didn't understand why they were taken in opposite directions. They didn't understand that by law, blacks were not allowed to attend schools where there were white students. They did not understand anything about segregation. All they knew was that they wanted to be together. They let go of their mothers' hands, dropped their lunch pails, and ran to each other crying and holding tightly to their friend. Neither one wanted to be separated. Their mothers forced them to go to their respective school, the school for whites and the school for blacks. The boys ceased to play together after that. Their mothers agreed that it was for the best. Soon the white boy moved away, and they never ran into each other again. What a memory that had to be of the first day of school.

Finding the Arts

Meeting other people became my mission so I went to the NAACP office in nearby Hannibal where I met Ms. Dorine Chester, who introduced me to several women in the Fannie Griffin Art Club. I loved the Club and the things they stood for, so I became an active member of the only art club for blacks in the Marion and Pike County areas. Segregation was still in full swing, and members took on the task of raising community awareness in arts as well as in education. Fannie Griffin, a prominent citizen and nurse, was born in New London, Mo., and she graduated from the Homer G. Phillips Hospital's School of Nursing. She came to Hannibal to become one of Hannibal's first two black nurses. It would take a book to write about all of the wonderful contributions the Fannie Griffin Arts Club made.

In the mid-1980s, I heard about a statewide arts conference that the Missouri Arts Council (MAC) offered, and I decided to attend. I was 47 years old and had never been to any conference prior to this one, but the Fannie Griffin Art Club agreed to pay my registration fee. I was beyond excited to have this new experience. I didn't know what to expect, though I thought I would view some paintings and drawings, with which I would have been perfectly satisfied. However, a wide variety of art forms were represented. The visual arts, which I expected to see, weren't just drawings or paintings. I saw and heard the famous, dynamic African American gospel singer Mother Willie Mae Ford Smith, who sang at the conference and had most of the room in tears. (It wasn't long after that she passed away.) "Mother" Smith had been the recipient of the 1988 National Endowment for the Arts' Heritage Fellowship; she appeared in the film 'Say

Amen, Somebody;" and, along with Dr. Thomas Dorsey and Sally Martin, she organized the National Convention of Gospel Choirs. "Mother" helped Mahalia Jackson get on the Gospel map, and she is featured on the St. Louis Walk of Fame. Here I was, at the MAC conference, in the same room with her. Wow!! She was an icon who had touched the lives of a lot of people. The conference also included traditional and non-traditional musicians, dancers, and (oh-my-goodness) STORYTELLERS! Many of these artists also performed, gave workshops, and offered lectures at the conference.

Why had I been deprived of hearing about MAC until now? I was certainly glad I picked up the newspaper that advertised the conference. Becoming more aware of the range of the arts and making many new friends at the conference started a new growth within me. The icing on the cake was when I picked up a brochure about Missouri's Traditional Arts Apprenticeship Program (TAAP) offered through the University of Missouri in Columbia. I had been singing jazz and blues with Ben Bumbry and the Messengers, a Quincy, Illinois-based band. Here, with TAAP, was an opportunity for me to grow professionally and to learn with a traditional master jazz and blues vocalist. The possibilities gave me goosebumps. I called Dr. Dana Everts-Boehm, then-Director of the Missouri Folk Arts Program, who was very gracious and encouraged me to apply. She explained that TAAP was "designed to honor traditional artists and help perpetuate the traditional arts in our state by encouraging master artists to pass on their skills to committed apprentices." Everts-Boehm discussed the application process with me, and Ms. Mae Wheeler, a well-known traditional jazz and blues singer, agreed to apply as my teacher. We drafted a training plan and schedule, made tapes of our vocal examples, and sent them in. We received letters later telling us that we had been accepted and could get started with our lessons for TAAP 1988.

That day, I must have read the letter about ten times. I cried happy tears; I held the letter to my chest; I was so very happy. Little did I know of the long journey of discovery I would be making with TAAP for many years. Here I was, a woman living in a small rural Northeastern Missouri town, on the heels of being involved in the arts on the state level. A notable, popular St. Louis master vocalist was going to teach me how to be a better vocalist. I was starry-eyed and somewhat in disbelief; I just couldn't wait to get started. I didn't even have to pay a dime for these invaluable lessons. Ms. Wheeler taught me how to breathe from the stomach when singing and how to connect with my audience. She taught me how to let the audience know what I feel when I sing. Previously, I was always fearful when I performed but sang anyway. I had a nice voice, but didn't know how to project it. Ms. Wheeler taught me how to project, and protect, my singing voice. She also taught me some history of jazz and blues music, a part of our culture, and she was one of its tradition bearers. She was in demand in the St. Louis community and whoever hired her could depend on her drawing a huge crowd. She was very regal with her appearance, always wore a flower in her hair to match whatever beautiful outfit she wore. How lucky I was to be in her presence, to have someone teaching me that was this knowledgeable, passionate and generous.

Every other week I would drive from Frankford and spend the day with Ms. Wheeler to have her teach me valuable lessons about jazz and blues singing. She would always fix me something spectacular to eat. Many times I would accompany her and perform in public. It was not unusual for us to be seen and heard at nightclubs, festivals, conferences and other venues. We performed our very own concert during the apprenticeship for an hour at Forest Park–St. Louis Community College. What a joyful day that was to perform at my alma mater, where I started the Bachelor's degree I finished at Washington University. What improvements I made in my singing and in my performances thanks to Ms. Wheeler and TAAP. To-day, I still sing with Ben Bumbry and the Messengers; my small world was becoming larger, and I am very, very humbled. Ms. Wheeler is gone from this world now, but she has a permanent place in my heart. I will always miss this incredible woman. She received numerous awards for her vocal ability and for giving so selflessly to the community. I will continue to sing and to keep traditional jazz and blues alive as long as I am breathing.

Finding My Voice; Sharing It with Others

Singing has been a part of my life since I was a child. I used to sing in the shower or while looking in a mirror, but my shyness kept my voice away from other ears. As an adult, I came out of the singing closet, but I was still shy. My training in the TAAP caused me to be more comfortable. However, something was growing inside of me that put singing in the background. Storytelling!

Storytelling was my first love. I had obtained some success at teaching professional development seminars and in-service workshops to teachers. I taught them to use storytelling in the classroom to achieve their goals and outcomes, and it was rewarding for me. Additionally, I was having success as a storyteller, selling out performances. Storytelling had become as much a part of me as breathing. It was a perfect time to pass this amazing art form on to others. Through the TAAP, I thought that perhaps I could become a master artist; I would teach budding storytellers how to value their family members and others and how to interview them to collect stories. My students could become better at this oral tradition. Four years after my own apprenticeship, I was awarded the opportunity to become a master storyteller in TAAP, with my first apprentice, Deb Swanegan, in TAAP 1992.

After our first year in the TAAP, which was magical, Deb wanted to apprentice a second year. I also found two additional apprentices to work with, Vivian Hawkins and Samuel Williams. Over the course of the apprenticeship, they listened to their elders and remembered stories from childhood. We had memorable times learning, listening to, and telling stories. I think one of the most valuable lessons I taught them was to document their elders by recording them. I didn't document my great-grandmother, and boy do I wish I had. Vivian Hawkins continues to tell stories, and Samuel Williams became a police officer in Columbia. He tells stories to those who are troubled and who may benefit from listening. I see both every now and then, and we are still friends. They have supported the storytelling conferences I have since organized, and both continue to support storytelling.

Deb Swanegan and I were honored to be among others in TAAP who were asked to perform at "Tuesdays at the Capitol," a special series in Jefferson City, Mo., co-sponsored by the Department of Natural Resources, designed to educate the general public about the cultural heritage in the state and the value of passing it on. Deb moved to Columbia, Mo., and I would often drive there to teach her lessons during our second apprenticeship. In 1994, I did not submit a TAAP application; I believed that Deb Swanegan should apply, and I didn't want to compete with her. She applied, and she was accepted with Sheila Plummer as her apprentice. I was proud of the job that they both did, and both still tell stories. We see each other every year at the St. Louis and Kansas City Storytelling festivals.

In 1995, I was again selected by the TAAP panel to lead an apprenticeship with both Mrs. Dorine Chester Amber and Mr. William (Jerry) Grimmett, local elders, as apprentices. Mrs. Ambers, born in Withers Mill, Mo., was a Paul Laurence Dunbar aficionado and storyteller. She taught me as many new stories as I taught her about the art of storytelling, and she started performing in public shortly after our apprenticeship ended. One of the stories Mrs. Ambers told me was about an incident that occurred when she worked at the Hannibal Country Club, which didn't allow blacks in their facilities at the time. However, blacks were allowed to cook for the whites that frequented the club. The cooks and servers were under strict rules not to eat there, to enter from the back, and to stay in the back at all times. One year, when planning a high school graduation party, the white graduating students insisted on bringing their black fellow graduating classmate, Larry Thompson. Some parents objected to a black person gracing their prestigious country club. The classmates wouldn't give in and refused to have the party there unless Larry could attend. The parents finally relented, and the party was held at the country club. There were no incidents, and it was a success. Larry didn't bite or do whatever horrible thing they expected a black graduating young man to do. He went on to enjoy a very prominent position. [Mrs. Ambers would have had a big smile on her face had she been here on March 10, 2001 when Larry Thompson was appointed Deputy Attorney General to the United States. That is quite an accomplishment for the person who caused grown people unnecessary fear.]

Mr. Grimmett, my second apprentice that year, was a walking, talking history book. The subject he talked about most was his family, especially his daughters Dawn and Brenda (who lost her life after a lengthy battle with lupus.) He was a kind man who overcame many obstacles. He was always armed with two pieces of paper—his birth certificate which identified him as "no name Grimmett" and his "Honorable Discharge" certificate from the Colored Civilian Conservation Corps on March 25, 1941. Mr. Grimmett often told stories in schools concerning his life, and students couldn't get enough of his storytelling. He joined the US Army in 1943 where he served until 1945. He was awarded two Bronze Stars for his campaigns in Normandy and northern France, among other awards, and he was an expert rifleman. When the Missouri Folk Arts Program sent an outside evaluator to observe our apprenticeship, she really got an earful with stories about his slave ancestors; his grandmother's midwifery; and Mr. Grimmett's own occupational and military history.

The apprenticeship with Ms. Amber, Mr. Grimmett, and myself offered an occasion for the Missouri Folk Arts Program Director Dana Everts-Boehm to conduct research for an annual publication called *Missouri Masters and Their Traditional Arts*. We were able to introduce Everts-Boehm to local culture bearers who knew the history of Northeast Missouri's African-American communities, and she documented these stories with recordings and photographs. She interviewed local pastors, adults who had attended segregated schools, and local history buffs. The essay, "A Handful of Dinky: African American Storytelling in Missouri," covers the history of African-American settlement in Missouri, whether forced by slaveowners or voluntarily new Missourians like myself (1992). Everts-Boehm covered my family history and growth as a storyteller, as well as the residents and stories that I was helping to document in the region, including the history of an African-American community dubbed "Little Africa" near the town of Louisiana, Mo. Everts-Boehm's essay, in the book *Missouri's Black Heritage* (1980), and my own book *Stories from the Heart: Missouri's African American Heritage* (2009) all helped to document "Little Africa" and other African-American oral stories that might have been lost.

In addition to collecting and documenting stories, I was also storytelling at events for the public, as well as events in the schools. Storytelling, and the outstanding results it can have on an audience, never ceases to amaze me. I remember very vividly performing at an elementary school in Missouri and asking for volunteers to take part; students enjoy participating in the stories. There are always more than enough hands that go up showing their willingness to volunteer. This day, I couldn't convince anyone to volunteer to take the singing part in my story. I chose a young man to do this, and I trusted my instincts in doing so, but the reaction of almost everyone in the room caused me to wonder if I had done the right thing. When the young man came to the front of the auditorium, the teachers were in disbelief. They looked as if I shouldn't have chosen him. Students were elbowing each other and snickering. The student I chose seemed pleased that I chose him, and when it was time for him to sing the song that I taught him, he surprised everyone. This student's voice was so beautiful, and he appeared to be very confident. It was a most gratifying moment for me, a glorious moment.

Looking out at their reaction, I could see that some of the teachers had tears in their eyes, After the performance, the students who were snickering prior to his singing gave him a standing ovation as they cheered loudly. I told the teachers afterward what a terrific job he had done. They agreed and told me that they had no idea he could sing. Both of his parents were deaf, and he spoke to them in sign language. He had always been quiet in school and didn't associate with any of the students. He was "a very good boy." In reality, this gifted sixth grader could have fallen through the cracks. He was invisible to everyone. They could not "see" beyond his exterior demeanor to that which was struggling to come out, be seen, and be heard. They didn't really know him. Then along came a storytelling event that changed the boy's life. It reaffirmed mine also. That summer I was performing at the folklife festival in Florida, Mo. This same boy and both of his parents were in the audience. He later introduced us and said that after our storytelling session in his school, he joined the glee club. He said that he had believed that no one cared about what he could do. He felt it was best if he kept to himself. That day at his school, however, he took a chance, and he said he was glad he did. He signed that his parents thanked me for choosing him.

Finding New Opportunities

All of my opportunities as a storyteller, from professional development and apprenticeships to public performances in Missouri, led me to new opportunities that I never imagined. For instance, in 1997, I traveled to China with sixty-three other members of the National Storytelling Network's Education & Storytelling Delegation to the People's Republic of China. Me, going to China. I was beside myself with joy. Our local Toastmasters toasted me with a surprise going away party and another club raised some of my travel money. With the help of an interpreter, I told one of my favorite tales, "Why the Eagle Has a Bald Head," to a group of Chinese teachers. My great-grandmother told me that story numerous times, and I've been telling it since 1979 to anyone who would listen because I find it to be so poignant in my life. My visit to China was so surreal. Next to being in TAAP, getting married and giving birth to my son, that trip was one of most exciting times of my life.

The very next year, I was featured at the National Storytelling Conference in Kansas City, Mo., and about a month later, I was invited to be a featured teller at the National Storytelling Network's conference in Jonesborough, Tennessee where over 2,000 people came to my performance tent that evening. They gave me a standing ovation as I concluded another favorite family tale, "The Wooden Leg," a story about my Aunt Lou and her prosthetic leg. I was grateful for the opportunity to perform at this most prestigious event in the storytelling world, but almost didn't go because my then-husband Truman was in the hospital at the time. The doctor told me there was nothing I could do if I stayed and that Truman would be there when I returned. While I was very torn, storytellers and longtime friends Joyce Slater and Geneva Greenfield told me this was an opportunity of a lifetime and begged me not to blow my chance. They even said they would drive me there. At 5:00 a.m., on October 3, 1998, we were on our way to Jonesborough, where I performed. Little did I know that I was to return in 2003. I remember thinking again, "this can't be true." Tellers were required to have at least thirty stories in their repertoire and were not allowed to tell the same story twice. I was so happy; the audience members laughed and cried at my stories. On the final morning, a Sunday, I had to perform a spiritual story. My mother had passed away earlier that year, and I chose to tell stories about her and to sing a couple of songs. Almost the entire audience cried. There was so much love, and the crowd didn't want me to leave. I couldn't have dreamed of a more rewarding life. I believe it was all because I had picked up a brochure about the TAAP program at the MAC's Art Conference. Shortly after the end of the storytelling conference, I received a third invitation to be a featured storyteller and perform at the International Storytelling Center in Jonesborough. Of course, I accepted.

Back in Missouri, I was invited to be a presenter and performer at storytelling conferences. Evelyn Pulliam, who was my apprentice, gave me lots of work in Kennett, where I often visited the schools and nearby Caruthersville to teach holistic teaching/learning through the art of storytelling to teachers. Soon my calendar was full of jobs in the southeast Missouri region. They were six-hour drives one way. Evelyn was working for the library then, and I met numerous authors and teachers who were beneficial to my career. Those trips to Missouri's "Bootheel" led to another opportunity with the Missouri Folk Arts Program, when I was invited to be a member of the field research team assembled to conduct a survey of traditional arts and artists. I worked alongside oral historians, folklorists, and photographers, as we traveled around the region to interview storytellers, duck call makers, net makers, quilters, gospel singers, cosmetologists, politicians, farmers, chefs/cooks, and other community members. I especially recall that one of the foodways we documented was not commercial, but at a family reunion which had been held for over fifty years at the Cooper family farm. During the interview, Alex Cooper and Roy Cooper Jr. talked about their father Roy Cooper Sr. and other blacks who migrated to the Bootheel in 1946. Through a government program established after the collapse of the sharecropping system, Roy Cooper Sr. obtained the family farm, which still remains in the family today. Alex Cooper himself is an oral historian and storyteller of the events significant to the African American community with his own radio program based on interviews with local elders. Our research team also interviewed folks in such places as Hayti Heights, Caruthersville, Wardell, Sikeston, Malden, Kennett and additional small towns in the Bootheel. The research culminated in a public roundtable discussion in 1994, as well as publication of a resource guide now digitally archived at the State Historical Society of Missouri.

I was so taken with the region, I almost moved to the Bootheel. I remember meeting and interviewing a woman who was 99 years old, who could thread a needle on the first try without the aid of eyeglasses. She spoke of sugar trees and how the new construction killed them all. She knew the healing properties of those trees. I also met a man who told me he had built his house with his own hands, furnished it, and put two of his sons through college by cutting hair. He had a very successful barbering business for years until the government knocked on the door, telling him he had to stop until he went to school to get a license. He refused to go and started a career in carpentry instead.

By this time, I had also founded and produced my own storytelling conference and By Word of Mouth Storytelling Guild, where many storytellers in Missouri got their starts. I was also performing regularly at the annual St. Louis Storytelling Festival, and that is where I met my next TAAP apprentice: Loretta Washington! We exchanged contact information, and she accepted an invitation to my storytelling conference. As we exchanged family stories, I asked her to contribute to my next project (the book *Stories from the Heart*, mentioned here earlier). She accepted, and the rest is history. Her beautiful story "Ellen" is in my book, and Loretta tells it often at festival and public events. At this time, we also began to talk about the apprenticeship program, to which we applied and were accepted in 2003 with my second apprentice that year, Angela J. Williams. More than any other, Angela has become my most inspirational apprentice. We have traveled everywhere together, to Jonesborough, to visit professional storyteller Jackie Torrence in North Carolina, and to Jefferson City in 2005 when then-Governor Matt Blunt presented me with the Missouri Arts Council's award for "Individual Artist." Once again, I was pinching myself, not believing it was real.

Angela Williams is from the largest family in Hannibal, and I've known her since she was nine years old. Back then, I was hired to tell stories at her school several times. We reconnected when I saw her performing at a Juneteenth celebration, and she agreed to become my apprentice, despite a history of shyness. During our lessons, I had to let her go into my dining room and close the door in order for her to tell a story to the tape recorder; Angela was that shy. However, I could see something in her that she couldn't. As she told more and more, I recommended her for festivals, just as I had with my other apprentices. She began to elevate her voice and to make moves depicting the emotions of her characters. Additionally, Angela has been the sweetest, most open person I have ever known. I am forty-one years her senior, but she takes care of me anyway. We have developed a mother/daughter relationship although I could be Angela's grandmother.

Finding My Voice, Again

I am a stroke survivor. I came back from being disfigured, unable to speak, and unable to recall memories; I could have been that way for the remainder of my life. Just before the stroke, I was becoming internationally known as a storyteller. I had invitations from all over. My calendar was full.

A newspaper reporter had called from South Carolina to interview me to promote a performance scheduled there the following week, but I couldn't understand why I had difficulty answering her questions. When I attempted to pull myself together to answer what were very familiar questions, things got worse. I did manage to ask her if she would call me back. She said yes, but if she did, I was in the hospital. The next thing I knew, on March 11, 2005 (just weeks after the Missouri Arts Awards), I was in the hospital in Louisiana, Mo. for ten hours before they finally took me to Hannibal. I don't know why they didn't take me sooner. After an MRI, the doctor said that I had suffered a stroke. I knew he must be wrong. Angela came to the hospital that same night. I couldn't understand why she looked so worried. Where was her pretty smile? Yes, my face was disfigured; one of my arms didn't move where I wanted it to; and I couldn't walk, but I knew that was just temporary. A stroke was a foreign word to me. I knew I didn't have one.

A few days passed before I would give my consent to go to Rusk Rehabilitation Center in Columbia, Mo. I was determined to show everyone that I didn't have a stroke, but two weeks after the first stroke, I suffered another one. I had to be sent to the hospital again. The journey back to normalcy was uncertain at best and very difficult. Everything I knew was at risk–my identity, skills, hopes and dreams. I have never been so low in my life. I didn't know what I was going to do. The only thing that cheered me up was the many cards I received from fellow storytellers, friends, and family. Little did I know just how much the MFAP staff members would be my guardian angels.

Folk Art Specialist Deb Bailey, who I'd now known for over a decade, came to the hospital often to see me. She brought me flowers and storytelling puppets, among other presents. She was so good to me because I didn't know what to do. I was plumb out of my head. She helped me fill out medical and financial forms to get the services I needed. Deb even drove to Bowling Green, Mo. to take care of some business there for me. MFAP Director Lisa Higgins came to the hospital to see me also. Angela Williams drove from Hannibal to Columbia to the hospital almost every day. She would wash me, take care of my hair, and provide anything else I needed. I can't say enough about Angela because she helped to take care of me then and she helps to take care of me now. She herself has a very full life, as both mother and father to her son DeVonte, Special Education teacher, and barber.

Still to this day, Angela makes sure I go to doctors' appointments and to wherever else I need to be. I always expect her to put me in a nursing home because a person can only do so much. I didn't think I would be any good after my stroke. I came home in a wheelchair and for a while I couldn't walk. As time passed, my physical therapist suggested I go to water aerobics at the YMCA. On my first day of water aerobics, I had to be put on the lift to be let down into the water. I had to get out of the water the same way. I was so depressed that I stopped eating. Thinking something else was wrong with me my former husband took me to the doctor, who ran multiple tests and when he got the results, said that I was very depressed. Within a few weeks I got a bill for my depression. The bill was $1,800.00 dollars. That cured my depression right away. It wasn't long before I was getting in and out of the swimming pool without a lift.

Since then, I have participated in numerous public folklore projects, especially through the Missouri Folk Arts Program. In 2008, the MFAP successfully nominated me for a Fund for Folk Culture Artist Support grant, which supported completion of *Stories from the Heart*, with the assistance and encouragement of Rebecca Schroeder, long-time editor for the University of Missouri Press's Heritage Readers Series, and a foreword by Lisa L. Higgins. Later, I joined Missouri's Community Scholars Network in 2011, and in the spring of 2012, Angela Williams and I worked with MFAP staff to coordinate local logistics for an intermediate workshop in Hannibal, where we helped arrange field trips to local cultural organizations and sites. These include the Mark Twain Boyhood Home and Museum; Jim's Journey: The Huck Finn Freedom Center; Margretta's Beauty Salon; and the Eighth and Center Street Missionary Baptist Church.

MFAP staff also took the lead to coordinate a school residency project. Angela Williams and I taught students about storytelling at two Columbia, Mo. elementary schools, in conjunction with Black Women and the Stories They Tell, a special exhibition at the Museum of Art and Archaeology. MFAP staff has been one of my rocks in the time of a storm, recruiting me for projects, asking me to serve on review panels, and providing support for a Missouri storytelling documentary project that Angela and I dreamed of. I've been the recipient of many awards, including the 2005 Griot Award for Storytelling from the St. Louis Black History Museum; the 2010 Outstanding Achievement in Literature Award from the Missouri Humanities Council ; and, most recently, a Honorary Doctorate from the University of Missouri-St. Louis in 2015. There are so many more, but as you can see it all began because of public folklore projects supported by the Missouri Arts Council, especially the Traditional Arts Apprenticeship Program. I found my place and my voice, and it all happened in Missouri.

Reflections on Public Folklore: A Discussion with Howard Marshall
By Tracy Anne Travis

Dr. Howard Wight Marshall is Professor Emeritus of the Department of Art History and Archaeology at University of Missouri (Columbia) and founding director of the Missouri Cultural Heritage Center. In this interview, Dr. Marshall discusses his perspective on over forty years of public folklore, some of his formative experiences in "the field," and his continued work. The interview took place on his farm near Fulton, Missouri, on July 1st, 2016; numerous edits have been made to the recorded interview, in the interest of brevity and clarification.

Travis: I'd like to hear about your perspective on public folklore.

Marshall: I've never been comfortable about people saying that, if you're a classroom professor or academic, you're not doing public work. I think in some ways you are, and perhaps you don't see it. I've done a lot of different things in my career, in addition to being a university professor. Going back to the Sixties, it's been important for me to speak for the people whose work and lives I study.

But just about any time I would do any serious work, I would try to figure out how to go back to that town to present a program at the public library, or historical society meeting, or local museum, get an article into the local newspaper, or perhaps lead a discussion in a class, that sort of thing. I just always have done that. That's kind of how I was raised; my mother was a writer and a local historian, and she always said that if you learn something about people in your research, it's important to share it with people as many ways as you can.

Howard Marshall.
Photo by Nicholas Benner for University of Missouri.
Reproduced with the permission of University of Missouri.

Travis: It sounds like you're defining public folklore, as multifaceted … . People make that distinction between Academic and Public folklore, and you hinted that doesn't make sense?

Marshall: Well, it doesn't for me. It does for a lot of people. When I went to grad school at Indiana–this was in 1970, before even the term *applied folklore* was being used much. This is before the public sector had really developed as part of the discussion in academic settings, before the American Folklife Center, before the Smithsonian festivals had become professional and curatorial, and so on. At Indiana, Richard Mercer Dorson, the famous author and scholar, was the director of the Folklore Institute; he had established the institute. Dorson was an amazing scholar of the Old School. I mean, just the best you'd ever find. And I really liked him; I did well with him, and he encouraged me.

But the real reason I went to Indiana was because of Henry Glassie. Henry was breaking new ground in new approaches to the study of material culture and folk architecture; his 1968 book had been shown to me when I was working part-time at the Missouri State Park Board historic preservation office in Columbia, as a senior in college at MU in 1969. And that book (*Pattern in the Material Folk Culture of the Eastern United States*) just swept me off my feet. It was about the Eastern United States–buildings mostly, and very interdisciplinary. And I said to myself, "whatever that is, that's what I want to do." "Well," I thought, "if I can get into the graduate program at this Folklore Institute—whatever that is—that's where Glassie is teaching. That's what I want to do." And that's what I did.

And after grad school, I took jobs at the Country Music Hall of Fame, then the Conner Prairie Pioneer Settlement (an outdoor museum in Indiana), the American Folklife Center in the Library of Congress, then taught folklore courses a year at Kansas State before coming back to MU in 1982. The K-State teaching job was the only one considered strictly academic, but, even so, I did some public folklore while there.

Travis: What are you working on now and in the past few years?

Marshall: I published a little book with the Extension Division to see if I could roll my classroom lectures and research and books about Missouri folk building into a single, readable, small statement. So the little book, *Vernacular Architecture in Rural and Small Town Missouri: An Introduction*, is the result. I wrote it for the Extension Division, thinking that, with Extension's offices in counties across Missouri, the little book would be available to everybody. I gave away dozens, and I hoped that schoolteachers would find it useful in their Missouri history discussions. I like to think that book is another example of public folklore. We could go on and look at other books, articles, grant projects, museum exhibits, Cultural Heritage Center programs, and so on, and make a pretty good case for them being public folklore.

I retired in 2000, a long time ago, I appreciate the fact. There was an early retirement plan and I was in my last year as department chair and feeling burned-out, and I couldn't resist the offer. In retirement, I finally published *Barns of Missouri* (2003) and, and I did several other things.

If you study vernacular architecture (we called it folk architecture in the early days), it is in many ways like folklore and folklife studies in general: in conflict, or perhaps argument, with much of academic thinking about what's important in history and what's important to document and study and explain. You know, in your usual class on the history of American architecture, Frank Lloyd Wright is important; I. M. Pei is important. But as people like Glassie helped show us, how could the guys who built that common, old barn or log cabin somewhere be of any interest in the study of architecture? Well, those are the first people I'm interested in.

I dislike unnecessary jargon, but that doesn't mean I'm not interested in theory. In graduate school, I disliked the latest buzzwords in the hot theories and approaches to folk studies that were beginning to obscure academic writing, such as some of the French scholars' cultural linguistic writings. They are useful and intriguing ideas, but the jargon, and what seemed to me to be the elitist intellectual arrogance that came with the jargon, bugged me; [I suppose] it was great for the seminar discussions and the doctoral exams, and, no doubt, good for the mind.

But to me the jargon was useless when I was standing on a farmer's front porch trying to explain why I thought it was interesting to crawl around in his corncrib with a tape measure and camera. Jargon wasn't my thing, and perhaps that dislike of obfuscating technical language comes from my mother, the journalist, who wrote clearly and sensibly for anyone to read.

It's been interesting throughout my career, how to explain to people what I'm doing in their front room! "Why are you here? What are you going to do with this recording of my grandmother's recipes?"

And about the historic preservation thing, I can remember I started my first "public sector job" when I was back at MU, after getting out of the Marine Corps, and so on. Just by pure luck, the work-study assignment in 1969 was as a research assistant with the Missouri State Park Board's brand new office of historic preservation.

Travis: So that's what you were doing as your part-time job?

Marshall: Yes. And it was a new office, following the creation of *The National Register of Historic Places* a few years before, 1966. Every state had to get busy documenting sites and nominating them to the Register. Missouri's office was set up in rented rooms just off the University campus in Columbia, and a few brave souls were hired to figure out how to interpret federal guidelines, how to write Missouri's guidelines, to document buildings like log cabins as well as Harry Truman's big Victorian house in Independence. There was a lot of political finagling going on to get support from the state legislature as well as folks around Missouri on whose property interesting historical, architectural, and archaeological sites were located. Everyone in the office had to learn to explain clearly and convincingly the program's complicated policies and activities to anyone they met.

What to do about these historical things–how to record them, how to write about them, how to get them onto the *National Register...* . So I lucked into that as my part-time job; it could have been sacking books at the M Store, and it was a lot better work than my previous part-time carpenter's helper job nailing floor joists on a student apartments construction site. In the State Park Board job, I spent a lot of time as the field assistant for the office's archaeologist, doing fieldwork, talking to farmers about their Indian mounds, learning how to use various measuring devices of archaeology, how to use the big Graflex camera. It was quite an exciting experience. A good deal of this experience came in handy a year later when I found myself doing "fieldwork" for courses in folklore and folklife studies at Indiana.

I would find myself in a car with a state government license plate on a Ford station wagon, driving up and rapping on the door, and [the resident] saying "Are you Mister Marshall?" You answer, "Yes, I am." Then you hear, "Who are you? What do you want? Are you from the tax people?" You know, sadly, government of any kind and most Missourians don't get along, despite the countless ways government benefits them—and it has been like that since the Civil War and Reconstruction; but that's another topic entirely.

Anyway, I had to quickly learn to explain myself—why I'm in this government car, what's all this equipment piled up in the back, cameras, stuff. And the person at the door would know about it, of course, because we would have called him to set up our visit, and written a letter way ahead of time. But still, it didn't matter. You know, when you get there, you still gotta explain yourself all over again. I think that's what it's like for anyone in public folklore.

Travis: You mean showing up at someone's door and talking to people?

Marshall: Yeah. It's sharing, really. It's being part of a village rather than an ivory tower. That's what it's about. I can remember hearing in that office in Columbia one afternoon, 1969 or early 1970, discussion about a couple of the team who had gone off to record this amazing and very ancient barn down in, I guess it was south and west of Saint Louis. If you know that country, it's really famous for a kind of Germanic barn transplanted into early Missouri ... . Anyhow, the guys had come back from their trip and they were just kind of in shock. They had gone down to so-and-so's farm, and had obtained permission to record it for the state survey, and were excited to see the local landmark. They get there. And they drive up to the place, and they look behind the farmhouse where the barn should be, and there's a huge, smoking pile with odd bits of timber sticking up, the fire still smoldering. And the farmer said something to the effect of, "I'd just rather burn the thing down than have government people come out here and tell me what to do with my own property."

I don't know what the lesson there is in all of its layers, but one layer is, it's important that people you visit get some sort of appreciation that what they have is not going to be taxed, it's not going to cause them a lot of grief. Or their old ballad you want to record isn't going to be taken to Los Angeles and turned into a Kingston Trio hit record. If they don't want to be quoted in your article, they don't need to be. If you don't want these photographs used in an exhibit or a publication, they won't be. On and on, you have to learn this in your fieldwork, because a lot of people will do kind of what that suspicious Missouri farmer did, which is a dreadful thing, when you think about it—destroying his ancestors' prized barn to keep it from being—what?—by nosy government agents.

So, how do you present your mission as a student of cultural heritage? I've knocked on people's doors a lot of places, from California and Scotland and Italy and hundreds of places in Missouri. Time and time again it has proven valuable to be completely blunt and honest with people about why you're there. And if you can make a self-effacing joke, you know, on where you're from, you know, something like that's fine, to help break the ice. The more self-effacing humor you can use, the better. Because humor, a bit of a joke, is the great bridge between strangers, it allows for a lot of the heated air to go out of that balloon of distrust or nervousness.

Marshall: I did some contract fieldwork in the mid-seventies and early eighties for Ralph Rinzler for the Festival of American Folklife. These were bits of research, one year in Mississippi, and later in Missouri. There were some challenging occasions doing fieldwork for a federal government agency in Mississippi, and I learned a lot from the experiences. And later, during the years when I was working for Alan Jabbour at the American Folklife Center, we did many public programs and exhibitions, and a cooperative exhibition with Richard Ahlborn at the National Museum of American History in Washington ("Buckaroos in Paradise: Cowboy Life in Northern Nevada"), based on an interdisciplinary team research project that I had organized in Paradise Valley, Nevada. It was marvelous to work in the Library, and then to also do a few things with the Smithsonian, both of them government cultural institutions that do a lot of public folklore for the "increase and diffusion of knowledge" (the Smithsonian's motto).

Travis: I would like to hear about your projects now. Would you talk about that?

Marshall: Sure. Most of my fieldwork, research, public programs, and writing over the past twenty years have been in the area of Missouri's heritage of traditional fiddle and dance music. I can mention *Play Me Something Quick and Devilish: Old-Time Fiddlers in Missouri* (2012). That's conceived of as volume one of a trilogy. Volume two comes out in December this year, called *Fiddler's Dream*. And the same press, MU Press, will publish it, and it will also have a sampler music CD with it with a gob of Missouri fiddlers past and present. That 2016 book will take us from the 1920s to the 1960s. So, the third part of the trilogy will take us from the Sixties to whenever I stop typing, and that's the hardest to write because I lived that myself–from the folksong revival to now. Margot [my wife] wants me to write it more as a memoir, so we'll see if a way can be found to do that.

Speaking of public folklore, after *Play Me Something Quick and Devilish* came out in late 2012, I spent 2013 doing something like thirty-five presentations in locations across Missouri. When *Fiddler's Dream* comes out later this year, I'll begin doing public programs, especially in county seats or hometowns of fiddlers who are featured in the book. You know, the Press thinks of these things as book signings, but I sell very few books and I sell them for close to my cost. The point is, I'm bringing back and sharing with the community what I've documented and tried to comprehend about their history—in this case, fiddle music. And if you approach it that way, it's well worth doing.

In my programs with the books, it's important that people understand that these books are accessible to readers. You know, these books are not crammed with academic jargon and complicated theories. Close to the front of the book I say something like, "Warning: yes, I am a retired professor and, no, I'm not going to lecture you, and I hope there won't be any words you have to google." It'll be local history.

Travis: What other projects do you have going?

Marshall: Current projects? The second thing that you could say as a project, is that I'm trying to figure out what to do with all my stuff! You know, for many years I've given the Western Historical Manuscripts Collection various things, other things to county historical societies, the University's Historic Costume and Textile Collection, and other good repositories. The Manuscripts Collection has, really have, a lot of stuff on my family and ancestors, going back to the early times. But I'm trying to think about artifacts now.

One of the early fieldwork projects I accomplished—as an undergrad at MU in the Sixties—was to document a white oak basket maker, Earl Westfall. That undergraduate term paper at MU evolved into an expanded seminar paper at Indiana, and then a publication in *Mid-South Folklore*, a chapter in Jan Brunvand's textbook, *Readings in American Folklore*, and then the core of an encyclopedia article on white-oak basketmaking.

I'm a born museum curator and an artifact guy, so while I was visiting and documenting Mr. Westfall and his craft, I was buying examples of his different basket types and sizes. So, what am I going to do with those? Ebay? Yard sale? No. I'm talking to a couple of museums about donating the basket collection with my archival information, research, photographs, tape-recorded interviews, publications. And maybe, if they want, design a pop-up exhibit for them. In other words, give it to them wrapped in a bow. I hope that things like that can go somewhere where people will care about it for future generations. It's about the future.

I have gobs of stuff pertaining to violin history, too. I have probably half a dozen or more violins made in Missouri, mostly homemade fiddles that no collector or auction would care about, but they're interesting in their own sense of folk art, or whatever you want to call it. So what do I do with all those things?

And I do continue to play the fiddle every chance I get! You know, I host a fiddle-specific jam session first-and-third Thursday evenings at the Boone County Historical Society, in Nifong Park in Columbia.

And, you know, I have a fiddle student, one of the very few over the years that I've considered to be a real prospect to absorb central Missouri fiddling style and repertoire and maybe carry it on. The young man, Luke Cormier, happens to be the great-grandson of Art Galbraith, one of my early fiddle mentors and heroes from the Sixties. Later, as you may know, Art Galbraith was a teacher [in Missouri's Traditional Arts Apprenticeship Program] in the 1980s. I talk a lot about Galbraith in *Play Me Something Quick and Devilish*. So, this young man, Art's great-grandson, appeared out of the mist. He already knows how to play some fiddle, having had some violin lessons as a child, and he has a good violin he inherited. Amazingly, the lad is interested to learn what I can show him, and he seems to be as interested in the old stories as much as the old music. That's rarely happened before. It's exciting! Thanks, Luke.

About the interviewer: *Tracy Anne Travis recently completed her MA in the Department of English at MU, where she studied folklore and was an intern for the Missouri Folk Arts Program. Her research interests include historical reenactment, community healing from trauma, and old-time and Irish musical traditions. In her spare hours, she performs on baroque and Irish traditional flute.*

www.ingramcontent.com/pod-product-compliance
Lightning Source LLC
Chambersburg PA
CBHW051733020426
42333CB00014B/1289